Letts

GCSE EXAM
SECRETS

HISTORY

GCSE
Exam
Secrets

History

Andrew Matthews & Alan Scadding

CONTENTS

To revise any of these topics more thoroughly, see
Letts Revise GCSE History Study Guide

(see inside back cover for how to order)

SUCCESSFUL REVISION

Introduction

This book is designed to help you get better results.

▶ Look at the grade A and C candidates' answers and see if you could have done better.

▶ Try the exam practice questions and then look at the answers.

▶ Make sure you understand why the answers given are correct.

▶ When you feel ready, try the GCSE mock exam papers.

If you perform well on the questions in this book you should do well in the examination. Remember that success in examinations is about hard work, not luck.

Draw up a revision schedule

▶ Make sure that you know exactly what to prepare for, and which questions arise in each exam paper.

▶ Make a list of topics and be aware of which skills will be examined on each.

▶ Decide which topics to concentrate on. Look at the paper structure to decide this, as well as your own strengths and weaknesses.

▶ Spend more time on the topics you do not know so well: it is wasted on topics you do already know.

▶ Use the *Revise GCSE Modern British and World History Study Guide*. Use old GCSE papers and text books to help you to ask all the right questions.

▶ Organise your approach and cover topics thoroughly, one by one, over your revision period.

▶ Expect to spend about three months on revision. Your school will probably help you to do this by revising topics in the run up to the exams. Use this help wisely, by preparing thoroughly for school practice answers and making good use of the advice offered.

Revise intelligently

▶ Write your own revision summaries, with side headings, bullet points, highlighting, mind maps, lists of points for and against or any other technique that helps you to organise the material clearly and remember it.

▶ Concentrate on understanding each topic, not on just memorising like a robot. What you understand, you remember.

▶ Answer the type of questions you expect in the examination. This helps you to use all your knowledge and to identify any weaknesses.

▶ Take ownership of your revision plan. It should be something you do for yourself and not something you feel is imposed by others.

Don't do more than you can

▶ Revise regularly, but do not concentrate too long in one area. Vary subjects, or topics within subjects.

▶ Small doses of regular revision work better than last minute or late night 'binges'.

▶ Work intensively: stop when you're tired: switch off between sessions!

GCSE QUESTIONS

Different types of questions

As you go through this book you will see a wide variety of different styles of question. Each question is labelled according to the style of a particular examining board and a particular paper. Use them all for practice, but be aware which are relevant to your particular exam.

Specimen Papers for your own examination are available on the Internet at: www.aqa.org.uk, www.ocr.org.uk, www.edexcel.org.uk, www.wjec.co.uk, www.ccea.org.uk

Every examining board asks 'structured questions', i.e. questions broken down into several different subquestions, but even within one structured question different skills can be examined.

Make sure you know which kinds of questions will be asked in each of your papers. For example, one paper may include questions just wanting essay type fact and explanation answers, another may include source questions. Questions tend to fall into these two generic types.

Essay questions

▶ Essay questions are aimed at factual recall and your ability to write a reasoned argument.

▶ They will include several sub-questions, which may look at different skills, such as factual recall, the ability to explain the important points of a topic, or the ability to argue both sides of a controversial problem.

▶ They will not, as a rule, expect you to use sources provided in the exam. If they do, they will use them only to get you started on an answer that is substantially from your own knowledge.

▶ An important part of the marks will be allotted to fluency of explanation, so take care to spell correctly and construct your sentences grammatically.

Source questions

▶ These use short extracts from primary or secondary sources or visual evidence

▶ They expect candidates to evaluate the sources against the background of quite a good factual knowledge of the period.

▶ They indicate clearly whether the source or candidates' own knowledge should be used, and candidates should make sure that they obey the question.

▶ Some questions will expect the candidate to assess the reliability of the source.

▶ Other questions will expect the candidate to explain different interpretations.

▶ Some sub-questions, generally the last of the group, expect the sources to be used to make a balanced answer to a general question.

It seems to be fashionable for examining boards to include source sub-questions within otherwise essay-based questions, so beware!

HOW TO BOOST YOUR GRADE

The grade A candidate

▶ Uses historical knowledge to answer questions with consistency and accuracy, proving arguments with factual examples and making realistic judgements.

▶ Writes developed, reasoned and well substantiated analyses and will probably be able to relate arguments to other topics or even to events outside the course.

▶ Realises that causes are interrelated with ideas, attitudes and beliefs of that period.

▶ Can evaluate and use sources critically to reach reasoned and substantiated conclusions.

▶ Understands and can use interpretations in arguments.

The A* threshold varies between boards, but generally will be as far above the A borderline as the B is below it. In the past, History exams have suffered from a flattening of the graph of results beyond the A borderline because examiners have been reluctant to give full marks. It remains to be seen whether, in these new exams, that can be overcome. The result is that candidates need to be extra professional in their approach.

Given the high degree of skill necessary to reach the A threshold in History, it may be difficult to see how to improve far enough to gain an A*. To improve, the grade A candidate should:

In essay questions

▶ Look carefully at the question to make sure of answering exactly to the point.

▶ Take account of the mark allocation to decide how many points to make, and when to stop.

▶ Develop each point adequately to the task, but do not waste time in worthless description.

▶ Argue to a consistent quality, covering all relevant aspects evenly.

▶ Reason analytically, using factual description to prove points but not on its own.

▶ When giving reasons, relate them to the event you are being asked about.

▶ Comment on how convincing different arguments are, come to clear judgements which take into account the interrelationships between causes.

In source questions

All the above plus:

▶ Automatically include an assessment of the reliability of evidence in your arguments.

▶ Use sources and your own knowledge exactly as instructed in the question.

▶ Answer questions directly and with balance, rather than slavishly following the order of the sources.

▶ Understand and use different interpretations from the sources or your own knowledge around which to construct arguments.

Overall

▶ Be sure to give 'easy' questions their due – a mark lost there is worth just as much as elsewhere.

▶ Form a careful judgement of exactly what is required, rather than employing the 'scattergun' approach.

▶ Be aware that, as you will know a great deal about the course, time planning within the exam becomes even more critical for you. To spend too much time and space on one answer is foolish if it detracts from others.

HOW TO BOOST YOUR GRADE

Grade booster ···⟩ How to turn C into B

The grade C candidate

▶ Uses historical knowledge to answer questions.

▶ Organises the answer to explain or describe relevantly and can distinguish the key features or events.

▶ Evaluates and uses sources critically and can explain how and why events, people and issues have been interpreted in different ways.

To improve, the grade C candidate should:

In essay questions

▶ Look carefully at the question and understand what type of question it is.

▶ Develop the answer fully, using the mark allocation as a guide to how much to write.

▶ Show off all knowledge, but not to the extent that you exclude other important, relevant points.

▶ Be prepared to use all the time available to add to answers. Leave spare lines under each answer if it helps, so that you can add to them later.

In source questions

▶ Look carefully at the question and do exactly as you are asked.

▶ Evaluate each source in order to answer the question: what are its strengths and weaknesses?

▶ Quote directly from each source that you are told to use.

▶ Assess how reliable the source is by using your own knowledge or comparing it with other sources as well as from its own internal evidence.

▶ Never use a rote-learned answer such as: 'This source is unreliable because it is secondary.'

▶ Relate the authors of sources to their own lives: Who? When? Where? Why? To whom? Why would they believe that interpretation?

▶ Try to use as many sources as you can to answer general questions which ask you to solve a problem.

Overall

▶ Make sure of your own knowledge: revise intelligently.

▶ Write fluently and spell correctly.

▶ Keep a close watch on the time available and make sure that you can answer your last question fully.

Acknowledgements

p.8 (left) © Hulton-Deutsch Collection/Corbis; (right) © Punch Library; p.9 © The Imperial War Museum; p.14 top © 2001 Getty Images, Inc. All rights reserved; (bottom) © 2001 Getty Images, Inc. All rights reserved; p.15 © Punch Library; p.23 © The Imperial War Museum, London; p.28 © David Low, published in the Evening Standard, 15 February 1935, courtesy Atlantic Syndication, Centre for the Study of Cartoons, University of Kent; p.31, Punch Library; p.33 © David Low, courtesy Atlantic Syndication, Centre for the Study of Cartoons, University of Kent; p.41 © The Imperial War Museum, London; p.46, © Mary Evans Picture Library; p.51, © Yevgeny Khaldei/Corbis; p.57, © Leslie Illingworth, published in the Daily Mail, 6 November 1962, courtesy Atlantic Syndication, Centre for the Study of Cartoons, University of Kent; p.58, © Wally McNamee/Corbis; p.69, Robert Hunt Library; p.72 © Corbis; p.76 © David King Collection; p.79 top and bottom © David King Collection; p.80, © David King Collection; pp.87 & 89 © David Low, published Evening Standard, 03 July 1934, courtesy Atlantic Syndication, Centre for the Study of Cartoons, University of Kent; p.89 bottom, © Robert Hunt Library; p.105, Leslie Illingworth, published in the Daily Mail, 6 March 1946, courtesy Atlantic Syndication, Centre for the Study of Cartoons, University of Kent; p.106, © Wally McNamee/Corbis; p.107 left and right, The Imperial War Museum, London; p.108 The Imperial War Museum, London; p.110, The Imperial War Museum, London; p.111 bottom, Bettmann/Corbis; p.114, Peter Newark's American Pictures.

Britain 1906–1918

To revise this topic more thoroughly, see Chapter 1 in *Letts GCSE History Study Guide.*

 Try this sample GCSE question and then compare your answers with the Grade C and Grade A model answers on pages 10–13.

1   Study the Sources below carefully and then answer the questions that follow.

Source A

'Men politicians are in the habit of talking to women as if there were no laws that affect women. "The fact is", they say, "the home is the place for women. Their interests are the rearing and training of children … Politics have nothing to do with these things, and therefore politics do not concern women." Yet the laws decide how women are to live in marriage, how their children are to be trained and educated, and what the future of children is to be. All that is decided by Act of Parliament.'

(Emmeline Pankhurst, 1908)

Source B

Emmeline Pankhurst being manhandled by a policeman outside Buckingham Palace

Source C

Punch 1912, 'In the House of her Friends'

Source D

In Britain the first effective women's movement was launched in 1903: the Women's Social and Political Union. The suffragettes, as they were known, led a campaign to bring the issue of women's rights to the fore.

(Hodgson, The People's Century *1995)*

Source E

The women's suffrage movement has been portrayed as nearly moribund [dead] during the early years of the twentieth century until the Women's Social and Political Union brought new life into it. This view assumes the WSPU was responsible for obtaining women's suffrage, and places the NUWSS in the background. This interpretation underestimates the NUWSS's importance … although it was overshadowed by the more flamboyant WSPU, the NUWSS' transformation was one of the most significant developments in the suffrage movement between 1897 and 1910.

(Smith, A modern historian *1998)*

Source F

In some respects it was the most remarkable funeral procession London has ever seen. It was a tribute of women to a woman who, in their eyes at least, had achieved martyrdom for the cause which they all represent … No one would grudge to the memory of Emily Wilding Davison any part of that tribute of honour and respect which her fellow women Suffragettes have desired to render at her obsequies [funeral rites] … She was herself the most unassuming and the gentlest of creatures, though she possessed a spirit capable of heroic deed and sacrifice.

(Sunday Times, 15 June 1913)

Source G

Women delivering coal in 1917

Source H

Faced with a divided Cabinet, Asquith once again decided to refer the problem to other people, this time to a Speaker's Conference. The Speaker was still the same Sir James Lowther who was still opposed to votes for women. However, he set up a balanced conference membership including Willoughby Dickinson and John Simon who had close links with the NUWSS. The conference came down firmly in favour of the principle of women's suffrage. However, it rejected the idea of equal suffrage with men, recommending instead that there should be an age limit for women of either 30 or 35. In addition only women 'occupiers' [property owners] or wives of occupiers should have the right to vote.

(from Martin Roberts, Britain 1946–1964, the Challenge of Change, *Oxford, 2001)*

a   Study **Source A**.
    Why did women want the vote in 1908? Use the Source and your own knowledge to explain your answer.   **[6]**

b   Study **Sources B and C**.
    Is one picture more useful than the other to an historian studying the success of women's suffrage? Use the Sources and your own knowledge to explain your answer.   **[8]**

c   Study **Sources D and E**.
    How far do these Sources disagree about the importance of the WSPU? Use the Sources to explain your answer.   **[6]**

d   Study **Sources F and G**.
    Is one Source more reliable than the other about reasons for the success of the women's suffrage movement? Use the Sources and your own knowledge to explain your answer.   **[9]**

e   Study **Sources D and H**.
    Why do you think that these two Sources give different views of the impact of the different women's suffrage groups? Use the Sources and your own knowledge to explain your answer.   **[9]**

f   Study **all** the Sources.
    'The Women's Suffrage movement succeeded because of the First World War, and not because of the disruptive tactics of the Suffragettes.' How far do the Sources in this paper show why this interpretation has been reached? Use the Sources and your own knowledge to explain your answer.   **[12]**

(Total 50 marks)

OCR Style, Paper 2: 1 hour 30 minutes

These two answers are at Grade C and A. Compare which one your answer is closest to and think how you could have improved it.

Britain 1906–1918

GRADE C ANSWER

This answer makes a valid point from the Source, but James does not support it with further details from the speech, nor use his own knowledge to explain it in any detail.
3/6 marks

Photographs do not always tell the truth, especially when that truth is only indirectly relevant to the question. James has hardly touched Source C.
3/8 marks

A good answer should explain as well as just state the differences. It needs to go on to answer 'how far' they were different.
3/6 marks

The comment on each Source is correct, so far as it goes and both Sources are discussed, but James does not properly discuss the reliability of each Source, nor does he decide how relevant each was to success.
4/9 marks

James rightly points out that, because they were written for different purposes, the interpretations do differ. However, he has forgotten to point out that historians disagree on this point in any case.
6/9 marks

Where is the evaluation of these Sources? James did not even talk about the First World War, and certainly did not show any alternative explanation. This is quite a typical last answer, because the candidate has obviously run out of time. It is unwise to lose so many marks because of this.
7/12 marks

James

(a) They wanted the vote so that they could make themselves equal to men and put right what they thought was wrong. ✓ This speech shows that women needed to have a say in Parliament. ✓

(b) The picture in Source B is more useful because it is a photograph, which actually shows Miss Pankhurst being taken away by a policeman. ✓ It shows the way that Suffragettes upset the men. ✓ It is more reliable than Source C because Source C is just a cartoon.

(c) Both Sources say that the WSPU was important because it 'led the campaign' or 'brought new life into the movement'. ✓ Source D doesn't say very much else, but Source E says that the NUWSS was also important but it has been overshadowed by the WSPU. ✓

(d) Source F is obviously written by a man, because women weren't reporters in those days, ✓ so he wouldn't want to tell the truth about Emily Davison's funeral. Source G is a photograph, and it actually shows women doing men's work, so it shows they should get the vote. ✓

(e) They give different views because the television programme is for everyone, not just for historians. It would be boring if it said too much about the NUWSS. ✓ Source H is from a book so that the reasons can be written in detail. ✓ It's easier to mention different points-of-view in a book. On the television they just find one eye-witness to speak. ✓

(f) In Source A Miss Pankhurst explains why Suffragettes wanted the vote. ✓ In Source B she is being carried away after a protest, showing that the WSPU were disrupting life. ✓ In Source C we can see Suffragettes demonstrating in the background ✓ and Source D shows that the WSPU was most important. Source E shows that the WSPU revived the Suffrage movement. ✓ Source F shows support for Emily Davison's action at her funeral. ✓ So it's obvious that the Suffragettes were most important in gaining the vote for women.

Grade booster ⤳ move a C to a B
Candidates must write in detail to develop their points effectively. Quotations help because each one is evidence for the point being made and forces the answer to be relevant to the Sources. Sources must never be taken at face value, but must be evaluated: how far are they true?

GRADE A ANSWER

Nadia

(a) Although women could own property, gain custody of children after divorce and even vote in some local elections by 1908, they still did not have equality in any real sense. ✓ Their taxation would be managed by their husband, their wages (if any) were much lower than men's, ✓ they were excluded from most responsible jobs and were mostly dependent on men. ✓ Emmeline Pankhurst makes a good case, in Source A, by speaking as men usually did ✓ and limiting women's role to 'the rearing and training of children'. ✓ But she went on to say that Acts of Parliament decided 'how women are to live in marriage, how their children are to be trained and educated, and what the future of children is to be', which explains why women thought that gaining the vote would be a step towards gaining equality. ✓ In 1908 Women hoped that an Act would be passed to give them the vote that year, but it was defeated.

(b) Source B is a photograph of Emmeline Pankhurst being carried away from Buckingham Palace by a policeman. A man walks beside, obviously telling her to be quiet, ✓ while Miss Pankhurst is also obviously shouting (presumably 'Votes for Women'). I know that Miss Pankhurst was one of the leaders of the Women's Social and Political Union, the noisy wing of the Women's Suffrage movement. ✓ The picture is not dated, but there has obviously been a demonstration in front of Buckingham Palace and the men don't look too pleased. ✓ This is a primary source and it clearly shows the popular image of the Suffragettes, but it does not show how successful they were. ✓

Source C shows a classically dressed woman, holding the scroll saying 'women's suffrage' turning in alarm towards a mob of banner-waving girls brandishing hammers and obviously intending to do damage. I think that the first woman represents the hope of an Act to give votes for women, which in 1912 had suffered a setback ✓ when Asquith dropped the Conciliation Bill, leading to even more agitation from the WSPU. If the woman represents women's hope of the vote, then the caption 'to think that, after all these years, I should be the first martyr' shows that the cartoonist believes that the suffragettes' violence will destroy the chances of women gaining the vote. ✓ Though this is of the time, it is a cartoon, so it is not an eyewitness account of events. It is just the cartoonist's opinion of them. ✓ On the other hand it does show what 'Punch' thought – that the Suffragette actions were counter-productive and that the real effort to gain the vote should be through Parliament. ✓ This is good because it shows that the movement appeared to be split between the Suffragettes and the Suffragists and that many thought that the Suffragette actions were not useful. ✓

This is rather a full answer, but it shows that Nadia knows what is happening in 1908, to compare with the Source, and she uses quotations relevantly as well.
6/6 marks

This answer looks at both Sources in some detail, and analyses them well. It might have been more clearly expressed if Nadia had compared them more directly and had dwelt more on their relevance to the success of the movement.
8/8 marks

(c) In a sense they don't disagree, because Source D is obviously an example of the opinion that Source E is talking about. ✓ Source D only talks about the WSPU, and Source E complains that the suffrage movement was nearly dead before the WSPU 'brought new life into it'. ✓ However, Source E goes on to say that this 'underestimates the NUWSS's importance' which it sees as 'one of the most significant developments in the suffrage movement.' ✓ So they do disagree about the importance of the WSPU, Source D thinking that it was most important and Source E thinking that the NUWSS was more important. ✓

(d) This is difficult because neither of the Sources directly answers the question. The account of the funeral procession of Emily Davison certainly shows how powerful her martyrdom was in gaining support for the WSPU from the marching women. ✓ It was written by a man, yet in such a respectful way that it convinces the reader that these women are acting well. ✓ It is about the death of Emily Davison, run down by the King's horse at the Derby in 1913, so it's about something well-known. ✓ However, it says nothing about the actual reasons for passing the Act in 1918, five years later. ✓ Source G is a bit the same, in that it shows women doing men's jobs during the war: it shows them lifting coal and how dirty they got. ✓ It may be posed, but there is no reason why it should be false ✓ Everyone knows that women did jobs like this to help the war effort. However, it's up to the reader to connect this with Women's Suffrage and the passing of the Act. ✓ Each of the two Sources shows one aspect of the reasons for success, both are reliable in what they say, but neither directly answers the question. ✓

(e) Source D seems to come from a television programme, whereas Source H is from a history textbook. Both are quite modern, but I think the difference may be that the television series would be more for everyone and just make the main points. ✓ In a book you can write in more detail. In this case the book shows that the NUWSS had more influence on the important Speaker's Conference in 1917 than the WSPU, because John Simon had close links with the NUWSS. ✓
In any case, no one seems to agree on the importance of the different organisations. ✓ Obviously the Suffragettes in the WSPU would agree with the People's Century TV series, whereas the real reason may be different because it was men in the Speaker's

Conference making the recommendations. ✓ Source C seems to show that the passage of the Bill might be harmed by violent protest, ✓ but Source F is written with such respect that the reporter, presumably a man, had been affected by Emily Davison's martyrdom. ✓ Arguments can be made both ways.

(f) Source G shows that during the war women did men's jobs, and I know that they gained a great deal of respect for doing so. The WSPU had declared a truce when war was declared and asked women to do their bit. ✓ Source H shows the important decision being taken at the Speaker's Conference, which made recommendations that resulted in the Act. The Conference was in the middle of the War, in 1917, so that the War might have been important, but the Source does not say that it was. ✓

Most of the Sources offer other reasons for success. Source A shows an important Suffragette making her case very effectively. ✓ The same lady is shown being carried away in Source B after a protest. ✓ The television programme in Source D agrees that the WSPU (Suffragette) movement was most important, ✓ and Source F shows a reporter commenting on the respectfulness of the funeral and ends that Emily Davison was 'capable of heroic deed and sacrifice'. ✓ All these seem to show that the Suffragettes were important and had made people see that votes for women were necessary. I know that many historians do think that the WSPU was the most important reason for women's success. ✓

Source C seems to argue that the Suffragettes may ruin the chances for a Bill to be passed in 1912, suggesting that others (perhaps the NUWSS) were more important. ✓ Source E says directly that the NUWSS was 'most significant'. ✓ Source H shows that some politicians were sympathetic to the NUWSS (rather than the WSPU). So perhaps it was neither the First World War, nor the Suffragettes, but the quieter and more patient work of the NUWSS that made the difference? ✓

So, while the sources don't prove which was most important, they do suggest that there may be other explanations than just the First World War or the Suffragettes. ✓

Nadia has explained why the First World War and the Suffragette movement are important, and has then gone on to suggest an alternative explanation, answering the question directly. While Sources do appear to have been taken at face value, there is quite a bit of interpretation, e.g. of Source H, and Sources are put properly into their context using other sources and own knowledge, so some credit would be given for evaluation.
11/12 marks

Grade booster ⋯⫶ move A to A*

For good marks you must 'evaluate' Sources. This means you should make the examiner aware how reliable each Source is used in this way. There isn't time to write much, so you need to find a way to show doubts in a word or two. Notice how Nadia has used quotations as often as possible. It proves that the Sources are being used and is essential for high marks. Any question phrased as 'How far...' should be given a balanced 'yes and no' answer. Revise the areas in which historians disagree. Differences of opinion are essential in these types of question.

QUESTION BANK

1 This question is about pre-war politics in the period 1906–1914. Study the information below and answer the questions which follow.

Information
The Liberal Government of 1906 to 1914 faced many social problems, and especially the problem of poverty. They also faced political issues, including the demand for votes for women.

Picture of slum room

a) i) Describe the *poverty line*. ②

ii) Explain why poor housing was a serious problem at the beginning of the twentieth century. ④

iii) How successful were governments in dealing with the problems created by poverty by 1911? ⑤

b) i) Describe the methods used by the Suffragettes. ③

ii) Explain the reasons for the growth of the Labour movement during this period. ④

c) Did the Liberal governments deal successfully with their main political problems by 1914? Explain your answer fully. ⑦

WJEC A Style Question, Section B: 30 minutes

TOTAL 25

2 **Option D: Britain 1905–1951**

Study **Sources A to E** and then answer **all** parts of Question 2.

a) Explain what you can learn about poverty in England before 1908 from **Source A**. ⑤

b) Compare the reasons for the crisis with the House of Lords according to **Sources B and C**. ⑥

c) How useful is **Source D** for studying how Lloyd George acted during the crisis? ⑨

d) How accurate an interpretation is **Source E** of the real issues in the Parliamentary Crisis? ⑩

e) Following the resolution of the Crisis in 1911 by the Parliament Act, the Liberal Government met several important challenges before 1914. **Use your own knowledge** to explain how far the Government was able to deal with these problems.

Source A: Poverty in the East End of London in 1889 ⑮

Source B: The Budget of 1909

The requisite new revenue was to be obtained as follows. Death Duties were made to yield £2.5 millions more ... Tobacco was to yield £1.9 millions more, and spirits 1.6 millions ... Raising the income-tax from 1s. to 1s. 2d. would produce ... £3 millions; and super-tax was created for the first time, fixed at a low rate, and estimated to bring in from the incomes above £3,000 a modest total of half a million more ... But beyond them were others, not estimated to yield above £500,000 ... These were Land Value duties ...

Source C: Lloyd George speaking in Newcastle in October 1909

A fully equipped duke costs as much to keep as two Dreadnoughts – and they are just as great a terror – and they last longer ... Let them realise what they are doing. They are forcing a revolution, and they will get it ... The question will be asked whether five hundred men chosen accidentally from among the unemployed, should override the judgement – the deliberate judgement – of millions of people who are engaged in the industry which makes the wealth of the country.

Source D: Lloyd George as seen by Punch in 1909

RICH FARE.

Source E: Churchill's opinion on the Parliamentary Crisis, 1910, given in the House of Commons

We have reached a fateful period in British history. The time for words is past, the time for action has arrived. Since the House of Lords – upon an evil and unpatriotic instigation [scheme] – as I judge it – have used their veto to affront the Prerogative [right] of the Crown and to invade the rights of the Commons, it has now become necessary that the Crown and Commons, acting together, should restore the balance of the Constitution and restrict for ever the Veto of the House of Lords.

AQA B Style Question, Paper 2 Option D: about 50 minutes

TOTAL 45

1 a)i) Key issue: Recall and description of events and issues

EXAMINER'S TIP

Keep this short and to the point: a statement of fact.

The income below which families would suffer from hunger and destitution.

ii) Key issue: Explanation of key events and issues

EXAMINER'S TIP

Write in the form of reasons.

- Governments had not helped build houses, the population had been rising steeply for 150 years.
- There was a lot of poverty because there were no old age pensions or child allowances.

iii) Key issue: Analysis and explanation of key events and issues

EXAMINER'S TIP

Analyse by explaining what had and what had not been done.

- Much had been done: free school meals, old age pensions, fixed minimum wages, health and unemployment insurance.
- The reforms only covered the very poor. Free school meals could be provided, but often were not. Unemployment Insurance only covered certain trades. The Poor Law remained and people still had to go to Workhouses if they fell through the net.

b)i) Key issue: Recall and description of key events and issues

EXAMINER'S TIP

Choose good examples.

- Creating disturbances and shouting 'Votes for Women': chaining themselves to railings outside Buckingham Palace or 10 Downing Street; Emily Davison ran in front of the King's horse at the Derby; large public demonstrations.

ii) Key issue: Explanation of key events and issues

EXAMINER'S TIP

Reasons needed again.

- Real poverty
- Rising education of the working classes
- Poor working conditions
- Real injustice, e.g. Tonypandy

c) Key issue: Explanation, analysis and evaluation of key events and issues

EXAMINER'S TIP

There are three targets here, try to cover each of them.

- Certainly there were many successes, for example the change in attitude which showed that poverty was the Government's problem, leading to improvements from old age pensions, through free school meals to unemployment insurance. These became political questions, because they related to taxation and other compulsory deductions from wages. One result was the political crisis over the People's Budget of 1908, only resolved after the successful passing of the Parliament Act, 1911, which limited the powers of the House of Lords. In 1913 the Government had passed a Home Rule Act for Ireland, which appeared to be going to solve that problem. The huge season of strikes seemed to have reached its peak in 1912.
- While early 1914 seemed relatively quiet, but Sir Edward Carson was stirring up Ulstermen, the Triple Alliance of the Unions, in 1913, was likely to bring the country to a halt at any time, the Suffragettes were in mid campaign and so there was little prospect of political peace. The War transformed everything.

2 a) Key issue: Comprehension and inference from a Source

EXAMINER'S TIP

Don't just describe the Source draw conclusions from it.

- Poverty was severe: most of the children have bare feet, they don't look energetic and are probably hungry as well as badly dressed.
- Poverty was common: these people are sitting or standing in the open road, not ashamed and hidden away.

b) Key issue: Comparison of Sources to detect similarities and differences

EXAMINER'S TIP

You can comment on similarities and differences in what the Sources leave out, as well as what they do say.

- Source B shows how the rich were going to be hurt by the Budget because increased Death Duties, Income Tax and Supertax as well as extra taxation on tobacco and spirits, would hit them much more than the poor.
- Source C agrees with this, because it points out the expenses of being a duke, all of which would have been increased by the Budget. But it disagrees in that it goes on to say that it's the dukes who are 'forcing a revolution' and sees the issue as being 'whether five hundred men chosen accidentally from among the unemployed, should override the judgement … of millions of people who are engaged in the industry which makes the wealth of the country'.
- So Lloyd George thinks it is the Lords being revolutionary, whereas Source B shows the Government making changes.

c) **Key issue: Evaluation of the Source for reliability**

EXAMINER'S TIP

Certainly describe the Sources, but you must evaluate them too: how far is each reliable in the way the question asks for it to be used?

- The Source shows Lloyd George as a giant with a club in his hand, looking for Balfour, the Conservative leader, who is cowering under the table. Obviously Lloyd George wants to club Balfour with the Budget and eat him, captioned Rich Fare and obviously the 'Plutocrat'. This is a humorous comment on Lloyd George's anti-House of Lords speeches (such as Source C) in 1909. It shows how the Tory press thought he was acting irrationally in provoking the people to hatred, like the giant in Jack and the Beanstalk. But Balfour was Jack and would get out of the mess. It is good evidence for what one section of the population thought at that time, even though these opinions were later defeated, though it gives no detail at all.

d) **Key issue: Analysis and evaluation of interpretations**

EXAMINER'S TIP

Why did/do people disagree? Do the Sources show the disagreements accurately?

- Churchill was a Liberal MP and the cousin of a duke, so his loyalties may have been torn, but he explains that the real issue is one of democracy (the Crown and the House of Commons) against the House of Lords' right to refuse to pass legislation (veto). They had vetoed the Budget of 1909, making it difficult to afford the Liberal measures against poverty. The two elections in 1910, both returned a large Liberal majority, confirming the Government's democratic right to pass legislation. The new King, George V, forced the Lords to agree.
- This piece shows one point-of-view opposing that of the Tories/House of Lords which is unrepresented in this Source.

EXAMINER'S TIP

Don't just describe what the Source says, show whether it was a valid point-of-view at the time, and what it was arguing against.

e) **Key issue: Evaluation of extent of change**

EXAMINER'S TIP

In this case, the question centres on the extent of success by 1914. This needs a balanced answer in each area.

- The Budget had already been passed in 1910, but was followed by a period of very severe labour unrest. The worst point was a national miners' strike in 1912.
- Trade Union membership had risen from 2 500 000 in 1910 to over 4 000 000 by 1914.
- In 1912 the 'Triple Alliance' of railwaymen, miners and transport workers was formed to co-ordinate pressure against the Government.
- The Liberal Government acted quite well in the circumstances.
- They were sympathetic to Labour MPs and brought in payment of MPs in 1911.
- In 1913 they passed a Trade Union Act which allowed a political levy from members of Trade Unions.
- The Triple Alliance General Strike never came, probably because of the War, but the Liberals had acted wisely to conciliate, rather than to provoke the Unions.

To try to solve the Women's Suffrage question:
- In 1911 the Conciliation Bill was introduced but abandoned eventually in 1913.
- The Government passed the Cat and Mouse Act, further inflaming the situation.
- The death of Emily Davison at the Derby made the situation even worse, and only the War reduced the pressure on the Government.

In 1911 the agitation increased against Home Rule for Ireland.
- The reform of the House of Lords would have allowed the passing of a Home Rule Act.
- Carson was arming Ulstermen and collecting signatures for the 'Covenant'.
- In 1914 in the 'Curragh Mutiny' officers sided with the Ulstermen.
  Only the War had saved the Government from real trouble.

CHAPTER 2

The First World War 1914–1918

To revise this topic more thoroughly, see Chapter 2 in *Letts GCSE History Study Guide.*

 Try this sample GCSE question and then compare your answers with the Grade C and Grade A model answers on pages 20–22.

1 Look carefully at **Sources A to F** on the war at sea and the Battle of Jutland and then answer questions **a** to **d**.

Source A:

Table of losses in the Battle of Jutland, 1916

Losses	Britain	Germany
Battle and armoured cruisers	6	1
Old battleships	0	1
Light cruisers	0	4
Destroyers	8	5
Tonnage lost	117 000	61 000
Sailors killed	6000	2500

Source B: An official German statement about the Battle of Jutland, June 1916

The Kaiser addresses the crews of the German High Seas Fleet: The British fleet was beaten. The first great hammer blow was struck, and the halo of British world supremacy disappeared.

Source C: An American historian writing about the Battle of Jutland in 1964

Jutland gave no cheer to England. If not a defeat, it was a disastrous victory. The German High Seas Fleet had struck down 117 025 tons of British warships. The British Grand Fleet had sunk about 61 180 tons of German naval power. German armour had stood up better; German gunnery had shown itself more accurate.

Source D: A statement from the German navy from December 1914

As England is trying to destroy our trade it is only fair if we retaliate by carrying on the campaign against her trade by all possible means. By means of the U-boat we should be able to inflict the greatest injury.

Source E: Tables showing tonnage of British shipping lost and the average number of U-boats in action

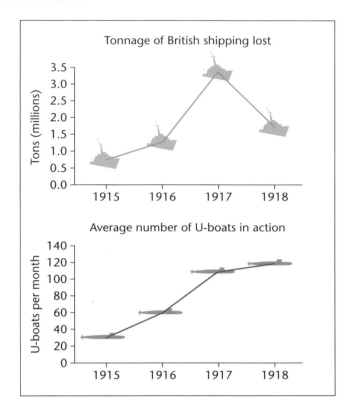

Source F: From a modern school history textbook

After Jutland the sea war continued below the surface. The Germans adopted unrestricted submarine warfare. They sank all shipping and it very nearly worked. In the Spring of 1917 Britain's supplies of food had reached crisis levels. Britain survived because the U-boats could not maintain their level of activity.

The British blockade was a key factor in the defeat of Germany. Starved of supplies the German army was weakened and the German people lost some of their will to support the war.

a   Study **Source A**.
    What can you learn about the result of the Battle of Jutland from Source A?   [4]
b   Study **Sources A, B** and **C**.
    Do Sources A and C support the evidence of Source B? Explain your answer.   [6]
c   Study **Sources D and E**.
    How useful are these sources as evidence about the use of U-boats by Germany during the First
    World War?   [8]
d   Study **all the Sources**.
    'Neither Britain nor Germany won the war at sea.'
    Use these sources and your own knowledge to explain whether you agree with this view.   [12]

(Total 30 marks)

These two answers are at Grade C and A. Compare which one your answer is closest to and think how you could have improved it.

GRADE C ANSWER

Emma has shown she understands the Source and has been able to draw relevant information from it. However, she does not draw any inferences or conclusions from this information.
2/4 marks

Emma's answer does refer to both Sources and uses some of the evidence to show support for the idea of German victory referred to in Source B.
4/6 marks

Emma's answer here gives a quite good assessment of Source E, using the content of the Source to show its usefulness, but also pointing out some of its limitations. However, Source D is not assessed well and is dismissed in a single sentence. The result is an unbalanced answer that cannot score very highly.
5/8 marks

When asked to examine two Sources make sure you try to say a number of things about each. An unbalanced answer cannot score highly.

Emma has gone through all the Sources and drawn conclusions based on the evidence of the Sources. There is some limited use of own knowledge, some attempt to show where Sources support each other and an overall conclusion is made. She has recognised that there is evidence on both sides. However, the answer is not well-organised and much of the information in the Sources is taken at face value.
7/12 marks

Emma

(a) Source A tells us that both navies had similar types of ships (battleships, cruisers, destroyers) and that Britain lost more ships than Germany (14:11). The Source also tells us that Britain lost more men than Germany (6000:2500). ✓

(b) Source A supports Source B because it says that Britain lost more ships and men than Germany and so Britain lost the battle. ✓ Source C also supports Source B because it says that German armour and gunnery was better than the British and that the battle was 'disastrous' for Britain. ✓ So both Sources support the view that the British fleet was beaten.

(c) Source D is not very useful as it only says what the Germans were aiming to do with U-boats in 1914. Source E is more useful because the statistics can be used to show how U-boats affected British shipping over the war as a whole. For example, in 1917 the Germans used 120 boats and sank over 3 million tons of British ships. ✓ However, in 1918 U-boats sank less than 2 million tons. So German U-boats were less effective in 1918. I assume these statistics are reliable. One weakness of this Source is that it is not clear that the first graph refers to British shipping sunk by U-boats. They could have been sunk by other things like mines. ✓

(d) Source A supports the view that Germany won the war at sea because in the Battle of Jutland, the only big sea battle, the Germans sank more ships than the British. ✓ Source B supports the view that Germany won the war at sea because it says that the Battle of Jutland meant that the British fleet was beaten and Britain lost world supremacy. ✓ Source C calls Jutland a 'disastrous victory' for Britain which suggests Britain lost in the end. ✓ Source D does not help answer the question. Source E shows that until 1917 Germany was probably winning the war at sea because it sank more and more British ships. In 1918 it sank less which means it was not winning in 1918. ✓ Source F says Germany was winning in 1917, but did less well afterwards. It also says that the British blockade helped defeat Germany. This shows Britain won the war at sea. ✓

Overall the sources show that Germany was winning the war at sea until 1917, but lost in 1918. In the end Britain won. This is supported by my own knowledge because the British sank lots of U-boats in 1918 and the German navy mutinied. ✓

Grade booster ····▷ move a C to a B
Emma could have improved her answer to **d** in two ways. First by trying to organise her ideas more carefully – dealing with evidence for and evidence against a British or German victory. This would help her to develop a more logical argument. She also needs to make more use of own knowledge to develop what is said in the Sources.

Dean

(a) From Source A we can learn about the types of ships involved in the battle, but more importantly we can learn about the damage to shipping and men suffered by both sides during the Battle of Jutland. On the basis of these statistics it would appear that Germany got the better of the battle because they sank more British ships than they lost and suffered fewer casualties. ✓ However, this does not mean that Germany necessarily won the battle, especially as we have no information here about the relative size of the two fleets or what happened after the battle. It is interesting that Britain lost more ships and men but we are not told why. ✓

(b) Source B is a judgement about the significance of the Battle of Jutland and comes from the German Kaiser. He clearly interprets the Battle as a German victory and one of great significance marking the end of British naval supremacy. ✓ To some extent both sources A and C support the idea of German victory. The statistics in Source A clearly show the relative losses of both sides and this lends support to the view of a German victory (Britain lost twice the tonnage of Germany and over twice the men). Source C confirms this pattern of relative loss to Britain and goes on to stress the relative superiority of German armour and gunnery. ✓ However, neither of the sources support fully the idea that the British fleet was beaten or that this victory marked the end of British naval supremacy. The statistics in Source A provide no evidence on the relative size of the fleets or of the effect of the relative losses. Source C, in fact, refers to the battle as a 'victory' of a kind for Britain, if an expensive one. ✓

(c) Source D is useful because it tells us of the German aims in using the U-boat – its main aim was to attack our trade. It also tells us that this was the intention from as early as December 1914. However, Source D tells us little about how effective the use of U-boats was in this respect. ✓ To some extent this information is provided by Source E which shows that the losses of British shipping were high, especially in 1917. The Germans in 1917 had declared unrestricted submarine warfare which indicates the increased effort made by Germany at this time to destroy British trade and starve her into submission. It also shows that this was the year in which a high number of U-boats were in action (120). Interestingly whilst the number of U-boats in action rose in 1918, British shipping losses fell, although the source provides no information as to why. ✓ However, it was probably because the British began to adopt the convoy system.

(d) Some of the Sources could be used as evidence to support the view that Germany won the war at sea. For example, the losses inflicted on the British navy in the only major naval battle of the war (Jutland) were much higher than those suffered by Germany (Source A), whilst the damage done to British merchant shipping by U-boats was also very high (Source E). Source F confirms the impact of the U-boat campaign by stressing how near Britain came to starvation in 1917, whilst Source B claims that the Battle of Jutland marked the end of British naval supremacy. However, it is difficult to draw the conclusion that Germany won the war at sea. After Jutland the German navy never ventured out of port again, and German naval mutinies in 1918 helped bring Germany to surrender. What is more, in the end the U-boat campaign failed as is indicated by the statistics in Source E – losses of British shipping fell dramatically in 1918 despite increased U-boat activity. ✓

There is also evidence in the sources which could be used to support the view that Britain won the war at sea. Source C refers to the Battle of Jutland as a British victory, although a 'disastrous' one in terms of losses sustained. Source E, as indicated above, suggests Britain was winning the war against the U-boats in 1918 – British ships were protected in convoys and destroyers, mines and Q boats were sinking the U-boats. Source F, in fact, indicates that the British navy played a crucial role in the defeat of Germany by blockading her ports, cutting her off from vital supplies of food and material. Indeed, it was the breakdown of German morale at home because of hunger and inflation as well as battlefield defeat that brought Germany to agree to the armistice in 1918. ✓

On balance, the evidence suggests that Germany, although it came close at times, especially in 1917, did not win the war at sea. She did not destroy the British fleet at Jutland and her U-boat campaign failed in 1918. On the other hand, although it could be argued in the light of this and the British blockade of Germany that Britain won the war at sea, the evidence is not totally convincing. On balance, Britain remained undefeated at sea and in this sense won the sea war. ✓

This is a very good answer. Dean uses both the sources and his own knowledge intelligently to examine the evidence for both a German and a British victory. He then comes to a balanced conclusion. The structure of the answer is logical and clear.
12/12 marks

Grade booster ⋯⋗ move A to A*
To score more highly, Dean could have made more use of the nature and purpose of the Sources in his answer to c. This is very important in questions which require you to evaluate source material. D, for example, represents a German view from the German navy which makes its usefulness as evidence of German aims more credible.

1 Study Sources **A, B, C** and **D** and then answer all parts of the question which follow.

Source A: A photograph of British tanks advancing in the Battle of Cambrai in 1917

Source B: A diagram of the cross-section of a trench

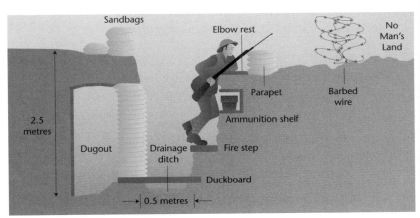

Source C: An eye-witness account of the effects of gas on the Western Front
We have heaps of gassed cases. I wish those who call this a holy war could see the poor things burnt and blistered all over with great mustard-coloured blisters, with blind eyes all sticky and glued together; always fighting for breath with voices a mere whisper saying their throats are closing and they will choke.

Source D: General Haig gave this view of the results of the Battle of the Somme after its end.
By the third week in November (1916) the three main objects with which we had commenced our offensive had already been achieved. Verdun had been relieved, the German forces had been held on the Western Front and the enemy's strength had been considerably worn down.

a) What does **Source A** tell us about the use of tanks in the First World War? ③

b) **Source B** shows a cross-section of a trench. **Use Source B and your own knowledge** to explain how trenches were used in the First World War. ⑥

c) How useful is **Source C** for explaining the effectiveness of gas as a weapon in the First World War. **Use Source C and your own knowledge** to answer the question. ⑧

d) Is **Source D** a fair interpretation of the results of the Battle of the Somme? **Use Source D and your own knowledge** to answer the question. ⑧

AQA Paper 1 Section B Style question: 35 minutes

TOTAL 25

QUESTION BANK ANSWERS

❶ a) **Key issue: Understanding of the information in the Source**

EXAMINER'S TIP

Keep the answer short and to the point – 3 marks, three points.

- Tanks were used with infantry.
- Tanks carried bundles (fascines) to drop into trenches to help them cross.
- Tanks were slow, moving at walking pace.

b) **Key issue: Use of Source and own knowledge to explain a key issue**

EXAMINER'S TIP

Make sure you use both information in the Source and your own knowledge. Make a number of points.

- Trenches were a kind of simple but effective defensive fortification protected by barbed wire and parapets of sandbags.
- By being below ground level and in narrow trenches soldiers were given some protection from enemy artillery and machine-gun fire.
- Soldiers in trenches could watch and fire at the enemy by standing on the firestep.
- In order to attack, soldiers had to climb out of the trench and through their own barbed wire.
- The dugout indicates that trenches were always occupied, day and night, and offered only limited shelter from the weather.

c) **Key issue: Evaluation of a Source for utility (usefulness)**

EXAMINER'S TIP

Make sure you refer to both the strengths and limitations of the Source by examining content, the nature, origin and purpose of the Source and your own knowledge.

- Source indicates injuries caused by gas (blistering, blindness, breathing problems).
- Evidence useful because it comes from an eye-witness of the effects.
- The evidence is about the use of mustard gas but other gases (phosgene/chlorine) used and had different effects.
- Source indicates that gas caused many casualties, but in fact deaths from gassing were relatively low.
- Source useful because it indicates gas was a frightening weapon (indicated by symptoms described here and the reference to 'holy

war'). This is confirmed by poems like Owen's 'Dulce et decorum est'.
- Source does not tell us the tactical purpose of gas use. Gas used to clear an area, but difficult to follow up because of impact on own troops.
- Source does not tell us about gas masks which were developed to counter effects of gas.

d) **Key issue: Analysis and assessment of an interpretation**

EXAMINER'S TIP

You need to evaluate the Source, test its interpretation against your own knowledge – evidence for and against, and draw a balanced conclusion.

- Haig believed the battle was a success because it achieved its three main objectives. It is true that by November the pressure on Verdun had been relieved, but some argue that the main pressure on Verdun had been overcome before the Battle of the Somme had begun. It is also true that the Germans made no breakthrough on the Western Front, but some would argue that was not their intention in 1916. It is also true that Germany's strength had been considerably worn down – the Germans had lost about 500 000 men and General Ludendorff believed the Somme left the Germans completely exhausted on the Western Front. However, the British and French had lost over 600 000 men in the battle.
- Haig's evidence should be respected because he was in a good position to comment on the battle as a whole as he was commander-in-chief. However, in this statement he could be trying to defend himself from criticism because of the immense casualties and the failure to make any significant advance. Certainly in the planning for the battle Haig had hoped for a breakthrough and had kept a large cavalry reserve to exploit any opening in the enemy lines.
- The judgement of many who criticise General Haig and suggest the Somme was a disaster often stresses the unprecedented casualties of 1 July. However, the British army learned much from this and were able to inflict substantial damage on German forces thereafter.
- Overall, Haig's judgement is a one-sided one which puts the best possible light on the outcome. A more balanced judgement would also stress the enormous cost of the battle and would question why it was prolonged until November.

CHAPTER 3
The peace settlements 1919–1923

To revise this topic more thoroughly, see Chapter 3 in *Letts GCSE History Study Guide.*

 Try this sample GCSE question and then compare your answers with the Grade C and Grade A model answers on pages 26 and 27.

Study **Sources A and B** and then answer the following questions.

Source A: Hitler's aims in foreign policy

Like many Germans, Hitler wanted to abolish the Treaty of Versailles. Germany had stopped making reparations payments. Now Hitler wanted other parts of the treaty changing as well. He wanted to expand German territory and unite all the Germans in Europe into one country. He wanted to expand German territory in Eastern Europe and Russia to create more Lebensraum [living space] for the German race.

(from a textbook published in Britain in 2000)

Source B: The Hossbach Memorandum

Hitler stated that Lebensraum for Germans was to be found in Europe. The first aim must be to overrun Czechoslovakia and Austria and so secure Germany's Eastern and Southern borders.

(from the minutes of a secret meeting between Hitler and his commanders held in November 1937)

a According to **Source A**, what were Hitler's aims in foreign policy?   [3]
b How did the Treaty of Versailles punish Germany?   [6]
c How reliable is **Source B** to an historian writing about Hitler's aims in foreign policy?
   Use Source B and your own knowledge to answer the question.   [6]
d Was Hitler's foreign policy the most important reason for the outbreak of the
   Second World War? Explain your answer.   [10]

(Total 25 marks)

These two answers are at Grade C and A. Compare which one your answer is closest to and think how you could have improved it.

The peace settlements 1919–1923

GRADE C ANSWER

Sarah

Sarah has made two relevant points, but she was asked to use the Source, and she has used some of her own knowledge, for which she would gain little credit.
1/3 marks

(a) Hitler wanted to abolish the Treaty of Versailles. ✓ He didn't like it because it showed that Germany had lost the First World War, and he blamed it on the Jews. He also wanted to take more land in Eastern Europe. ✓

Sarah has only mentioned one area of loss, though she has given several examples of this.
3/6 marks

(b) Germany lost a lot of territory including her whole empire, ✓ Alsace and Lorraine to France and the Polish Corridor to Poland. ✓

This would score well, because Sarah has given two reasons to disbelieve this source from her own knowledge. But where did the source come from.
4/6 marks

(c) This source is not completely correct, because Hitler invaded Austria before Czechoslovakia. ✓ It suggests that Hitler is going to war to take these countries, but in fact he negotiated control of both of them. ✓

Sarah has remembered the main events before the war and given two causes, which hardly connect to the events. A narrative answer cannot score well because it does not answer the question directly.
4/10 marks

(d) Hitler hated the Versailles Treaty because it showed that Germany had lost the war. It left a lot of Germans outside Germany in Poland and other parts. ✓ When he got to power, Hitler rearmed as soon as he could. Then he took over the Rhineland in 1936. The French didn't stop him. Later he took over Austria, because they asked him in, and Czechoslovakia. He got Czechoslovakia at Munich. He agreed with Britain that that would be the end, but then he went on to invade Poland. So it was because of Hitler that the War began and because Britain and France didn't stop him. ✓

Grade booster ⋯▷ move a C to a B
Answer directly. Questions for 3 marks may just ask for description, but for 10 marks the candidate must analyse, i.e. give reasons and argue which reason is most important.

GRADE A ANSWER

Dan

Dan has given four good points from the Source, rather than the three required.
3/3 marks

(a) To abolish the Treaty of Versailles. ✓ To expand German territory. ✓ To unite all Germans. ✓ To create Lebensraum. ✓

Good! Rather than just giving a list of different losses, Dan has grouped them sensibly, using the detailed provisions as examples of key points.
6/6 marks

(b) Germany lost territory: Alsace, Lorraine, the Polish Corridor, the Saar and Danzig (to the League) ✓ and all her colonies. ✓
   Germany lost sovereignty: she was unable to put soldiers in the Rhineland, ✓ her army was limited to 100,000 men, she could only have six battleships, no tanks or submarines. ✓
   Germany had to pay reparations: because she was declared guilty of starting the War, ✓ Germany was to pay £6,600,000 in gold. ✓

Dan has given a balanced answer, discussing the unreliability and the reliability. He uses the Source and his own knowledge. Lastly he evaluates the origin (provenance) of the Source as well as the content of it.
6/6 marks

(c) This extract from the Hossbach Memorandum is not very reliable. In the first place, it just gives one snapshot of Hitler's aims at one time in 1937. ✓ It does not even include the minutes of the whole meeting, so that it infers that Hitler was planning the War before it happened, whereas Hitler was as surprised as anyone else when war started in 1939. ✓ His plans were for little wars in the 1940s, not for a World War in 1939. ✓

However, the Source does show that Hitler intended to use warfare of some sort ('overrun'), ✓ and it predicted where expansion would happen first ('Germany's Eastern and Southern borders'). ✓ Hitler was talking in private with his commanders, so he was presumably telling the truth. ✓

(d) There were many other reasons for the outbreak of the Second World War. Certainly the Versailles Settlement created instability, since none of the Great Powers was prepared to enforce it, ✓ and it created hatred within Germany and the desire for change, ✓ but this could have happened peacefully. Neither the foreign policies of Stresemann, nor perhaps Hitler's earliest aims, would have created World War. ✓ There arose in the 1930s a substantial consensus of the Powers that revision of Versailles was necessary. ✓ Neither the Wall Street Crash, nor the failure of the League materially altered this, indeed they probably made it easier since the reordering of relative strengths and the end of the real responsibility of the Powers to maintain Versailles probably made war less likely. ✓ So why did war begin?

Until the end of 1938, Hitler had been remarkably successful in negotiating concessions, in the 1935 Anglo-German Naval Agreement, in the 1936 remilitarisation of the Rhineland and in the 1938 anschluss with Austria and annexation of the Sudetenland. ✓ The agreement with Chamberlain at Munich promised 'peace in our time'. Hitler had gained, through his foreign policy ambitions, just about as much as the situation would allow. ✓ But in March 1939 he began to overstep the mark – he invaded Eastern Czechoslovakia, taking over a non-German population. ✓ This was a significant departure from his previous nationalist aims and it provoked a flurry of diplomatic activity from Britain and France to reassure the nations of Eastern Europe. The alliances made at this time, with Poland and Romania, committed Britain and France to war if Hitler pushed any further. ✓ It spelled the end of appeasement, and was caused by Hitler's personal misjudgement of the situation, specifically his ambition to gain Lebensraum ✓ in the Ukraine. The alliance with the USSR just allowed Hitler the freedom to begin the invasion of Poland, a second instance of the same mistake. ✓

It was Hitler's aggressive ambitions that changed foreign policy from Stresemann's peaceful revision of Versailles to war. ✓ Even appeasement did not, in itself, create this aggression. The Wall Street Crash and the destruction of League power probably postponed, rather than brought on war. ✓ Even so, it was not Hitler's nationalist ambitions that created opposition, but his decision to push eastwards, create a border with the USSR and create Lebensraum. ✓

Dan has used most of the important causes for war, and has put them into context, while arguing that one section of Hitler's ambitions was most important. His ability to discuss different stages in Hitler's ambitions is interesting and would single him out as a high-achieving candidate. On the other hand his concentration on one line of argument was a little unbalanced. However, this is a multicausal, sustained and relevant answer and would clearly score highly.
10/10 marks

> ## Grade booster ---> move A to A*
> The directly relevant answer will always score well. Answers do not need to be wordy – you can list relevant points (as in the answers to a), keeping time in hand for the high tariff questions towards the end.

QUESTION BANK

1 a) What did Clemenceau want to gain from Germany at Versailles? ④

   b) Why did French and American aims conflict at the Paris Peace Conference? ⑥

   c) The Versailles Settlement satisfied no one. Was it therefore unfair? Explain your answer. ⑩

   OCR B Style Question, Section B: 35 minutes

TOTAL 20

---

2 **Option W, International History, 1919–1963**

Study **Sources A and B** and then answer **all** parts of Question 2 which follow.

Source A: Statement about the Versailles Treaty

We came to Paris confident that the new order was about to be established: we left it convinced that the new order had merely fouled the old. We arrived as fervent apprentices in the school of President Wilson: we left as renegades … We arrived determined that a Peace of justice and wisdom should be negotiated: we left it, conscious that the Treaties were neither just nor wise.

(from the diary of Harold Nicolson, a member of the British delegation at the Paris Peace Conference)

Source B: Cartoon about the League

(David Low, London Evening Standard, *15 February, 1935)*

a) According to **Source A,** how did the Treaty of Versailles fall short of the aims of the British delegation? ③

b) Why was Versailles ineffective in enforcing peace? ⑥

c) How reliable is **Source B** to an historian writing about the weaknesses of the League?

   Use Source B and your own knowledge to answer the question. ⑥

d) Was the refusal of the League to use armed force the most important reason for its failure in the 1930s? ⑩

   AQA Style, Paper 1: 35 minutes

TOTAL 25

---

①a) Key issue: Recall and communication of knowledge

- Security, e.g. demilitarisation of Rhineland.
- Revenge, e.g. war guilt blamed on Germany.
- Reparation, e.g. payment of £6 600 000 in gold set in 1921.

b) Key issue: Explain and communicate knowledge

- Because the USA had lost few men, Wilson was prepared to be fairer than Clemenceau, who wanted revenge.
- Because the USA disliked empires, they wanted them destroyed through national self-determination, whereas Clemenceau did not want to create a greater Germany.
- Because the USA was not threatened by German power, they wanted to keep Germany stronger to resume trade. Clemenceau wanted Germany left as weak as possible.

c) Key issue: Communicate through description, analysis and explanation

The American Senate was so disappointed by Versailles that they refused to confirm it. The British delegation thought it was 'neither just nor wise'. The French were disappointed that Germany remained potentially powerful, and invaded only two years later. No one was satisfied by the Treaty, least of all the Germans, who would not have agreed to any of the outcomes advocated by the Great Powers, since they all fell short of Wilson's Fourteen Points of 1917. However, the Treaty satisfied no one because it was a compromise between very different aims, and was skilfully negotiated to achieve something out of an impossible situation. A compromise peace was thought to be better than no peace at all.
Certainly the Peace was unfair to Germany, because Germany had lost the war. Even President Wilson supported justice less than he had before about 300 000 American soldiers had died. Clemenceau demanded revenge for the 1 400 000 French dead, which it was thought gave France, rather than Germany the moral right to demand restitution, because Germany had started the war and then lost it. Thus the Peace would be fairer to French losses than to German – it could never be fair to both. Equally, fairness was seen in the weakening of Germany's ability to attack France, rather in the application of the 'fair' principle of 'self-determination', which would have enlarged Germany by adding Austria. So the Peace was bound to be unfair to Germany.
Was the Peace unfair because it satisfied no one? No, because the satisfaction of e.g. French desires, could only be at the cost of being more unfair to Germany, and more disobliging to American aims. Equally the other way round. The peace which would have dissatisfied the Allies most, was to have left German power intact.

②a) Key issue: Comprehension of source

- Instead of a 'new order', 'the new order had merely fouled the old'.
- Instead of 'fervent apprentices in the school of President Wilson', 'we left as renegades'.
- Instead of a peace of 'justice and wisdom', 'the Treaties were neither just nor wise'.

b) Key issue: Description of key features and characteristics

- Because no nation supported the Treaty wholeheartedly enough to go to war to defend it.
- Because the League of Nations was sworn to enforce the Treaty, but at the same time to disarmament.
- Because no nation would willingly go to war after the First World War.

c) **Key issue: Evaluation of a Source for reliability in context**

This cartoon was drawn by a British cartoonist in 1935 and therefore would not openly accuse Britain of destroying the League, and yet Britain had assured Mussolini the year before that it would ignore an Italian expedition to Abyssinia. Low hints at this by showing Simon (Britain) and Laval (France) busily looking away from Mussolini. On the other hand, the Source does show the selfishness and self-interests of Mussolini, a good example of the self-interest of other Council members: France over the Ruhr, Britain over the Geneva Protocol, Mussolini over Corfu, Japan over Manchuria. This was the main cause for the destruction of the League.

d) **Key issue: Explanation of causation**

It would clearly have shocked Japan in 1931, Italy in 1935, Germany in 1936 and 1938, if the League had used force. If they had thought this a serious risk, they would not have contemplated their aggressions. Yet this argument is too simple, because Britain and France could not use force. They had been impoverished by the First World War and further by the Depression. They had signed up to the disarmament principle of the League of Nations at Geneva in 1933. Their populations were set against war, and they were democracies. The really great powers, the USA and USSR, were both isolated and uninvolved in keeping the peace. In these circumstances the use of armed force was impossible. There were too many interrelated problems in doing so.

The League of Nations

To revise this topic more thoroughly, see Chapter 4 in *Letts GCSE History Study Guide.*

Try this sample GCSE question and then compare your answers with the Grade C and Grade A model answers on the next page.

Study the Source below carefully, and then answer the questions which follow.

Source A: A British cartoon about the League of Nations from 1920

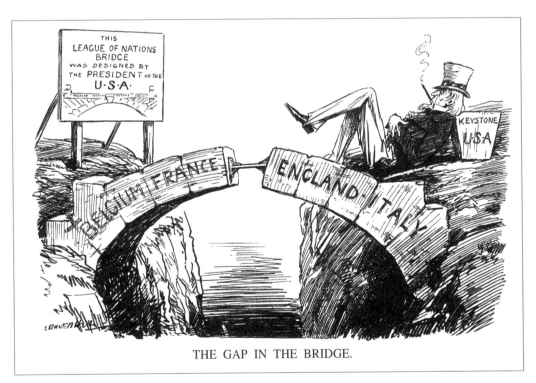

THE GAP IN THE BRIDGE.

a Study **Source A**. Explain the point the cartoonist is making about the League of Nations. Support your answer by referring to details of the cartoon and your own knowledge. [6]

b Explain the aims of the League of Nations [9]

OCR Paper 1, Section A Style Question: 15 minutes

(Total 15 marks)

GRADE C ANSWER

This is an accurate answer about the USA. Georgios has used his own knowledge to answer the question. However, this cannot score highly because he has not used the details of the cartoon to explain the point the cartoonist is making.
2/6 marks

Georgios has identified the main aims of the League of Nations and said something about its work. However, he has not developed his explanation by giving details of why the League had these aims and how it might achieve them.
6/9 marks

Georgios

(a) America was not a member of the League of Nations so it was weak. ✓ America was the most powerful country on earth. ✓

(b) The League had a number of aims. These were to settle disputes between member states, ✓ to keep peace in the world, ✓ to bring about disarmament and to improve the living conditions of people around the world. ✓ It set up agencies to help with the last aim, such as the International Labour Organisation. It also helped to return refugees to their own countries after the war and wanted to stop slavery. ✓

Grade booster ⋯⋯⋗ move a C to a B
Georgios could improve his answers by making sure in **a** that he responds to the instructions in the question which ask him to refer to the details of the cartoon in his answer. In **b** he needs to explain the aims he identified.

GRADE A ANSWER Julie

Julie's is a good answer because she has seen the main point of the cartoon and has used both the details of the cartoon and her own knowledge to explain its meaning.
5/6 marks

(a) The cartoonist is making the point that without the membership of the USA the League of Nations would be very weak. ✓ He does this by showing the league as a bridge made up of the major powers – Belgium, France, England and Italy. However, the keystone of the bridge – the USA – is missing and only a thin piece of wood is holding the bridge in place. ✓ This indicates the cartoonist's view that, without the USA, the bridge was likely to collapse at the slightest disturbance. Uncle Sam is relaxing against the keystone. This was probably to indicate that the American people did not want America to be involved in the League, ✓ which is why Wilson was not re-elected in 1920 and why the American Senate rejected the League. ✓

A sound answer here. Julie has identified and explained the League's main peacekeeping aim effectively by using her knowledge of why it was set up and some of the ways it could resolve disputes. She has also explained its wider social and economic aims with a couple of examples.
8/9 marks

(b) The main reason why the League was set up at the end of the First World War was to try and create a new way of resolving international disputes without going to war. Above all the organisers of the League wanted to avoid a repeat of the First World War. ✓ Some disputes could be dealt with by an international court set up in The Hague. ✓ However, the main aim was to use the League to resolve disputes – members could appeal to the League and, if both sides agreed, the League would make a judgement. ✓ If a member state was attacked by another the principle of collective security would come into operation. ✓ All members would come to the defence of the attacked state. This principle was set out in the League Covenant. The League also hoped to improve living and working conditions throughout the world through it's agencies, like the International Labour Organisation and World Health Organisation. ✓

Grade booster ⋯⋯⋗ move A to A*
Julie could improve her marks in the first part of the question by referring to the sign on the left of the bridge and making the point that the League was the idea of the American president Wilson (whose country then, ironically, refused to become a member). In the second part she could have explained a little more about the kinds of social and economic problems the League hoped to solve, or given examples of the type of dispute that might be resolved peacefully at The Hague.

1 Study **Sources A and B** and then answer the questions which follow.

Source A: A comment on the League of Nations by Mussolini, the Fascist leader of Italy
The League is alright when sparrows quarrel; it fails when eagles fall out.

Source B: A cartoon by David Low published in a British newspaper in 1932. It is entitled 'The Doormat'

a) According to **Source A,** when was the League successful and when did it fail? ③

b) **Source B** is about the effect of the Japanese invasion of Manchuria. Describe the main features of the Manchurian Crisis. ⑥

c) How useful is **Source B** to an historian writing about the failure of the League of Nations? Use **Source B** and your own knowledge to explain your answer. ⑥

d) Was the absence of the USA the main reason for the League's failure in the 1930s? Explain your answer. ⑩

AQA Paper 1, Section A, style question: 35 minutes

TOTAL 25

2 a) Describe how the League aimed to keep peace in the world. ④

b) Why did some major states not become members of the League when it was set up? ⑥

c) 'The League had more success than failure in the 1920s.' Do you agree with this statement? Explain your answer. ⑩

OCR Paper 1, Section B: 35 minutes

TOTAL 20

The League of Nations

①a) **Key issue: Comprehension of Source**

- The League only worked when dealing with disputes between minor powers (sparrows).
- It failed when major powers (eagles) were involved in disputes.

b) **Key issue: Description of a key event**

EXAMINER'S TIP

You need to get across the key points about the Manchurian Crisis.

- Many Nationalists in Japan and its army wanted to take over the Chinese province of Manchuria to provide land and resources.
- The Japanese army used the Mukden Incident in 1931, when it accused the Chinese of blowing up the Japanese controlled railway, as the excuse they needed to take over Manchuria.
- China appealed to the League, which did little except to appoint a commission under Lord Lytton to investigate the issue. Meanwhile Japan took over Manchuria.
- Lord Lytton reported in 1933 that Japan was the aggressor and the League told Japan to leave Manchuria. Instead Japan left the League.
- The League did nothing and so exposed its weakness – it had failed to stop aggression.

c) **Key issue: Evaluating the usefulness of a Source**

EXAMINER'S TIP

Use the details of the cartoon to help you explain what it can show about the League's failure. Comment on the nature and origin of the Source. Say something about its limitations.

- The cartoon is not a useful source of fact about the League's failure as it is intended as an interpretation of the League's handling of the Manchurian Crisis. It is in this aspect it can be considered useful.
- It is commenting on Japan's invasion of Manchuria and the failure of the League to do anything about it. The cartoonist is suggesting that Japan (a member of the League Council) considered the League of little account and treated it like a doormat. It is also suggesting the League accepted this role and was still happy to welcome Japan (the bowing doorman). Meanwhile, whilst Japan wiped its feet on the League, the

League tried to save face (hence the make-up) by requesting a report.
- The Source comes from a newspaper of a major member of the League (Britain) and reflects the growing disillusion with the League and its failure to do anything effective to stop Japanese aggression. The cartoon is a useful guide to the opinion of some people about the League.
- It is not a useful indicator of the opinion of all because the League continued to retain the support of many people as the main guarantor of international cooperation and peace.

d) **Key issue: Explanation of a key development**

EXAMINER'S TIP

You must write about the impact of the USA's absence from the League and compare its importance in explaining the League's failure with two or three other major reasons for failure.

- The League was severely damaged by the absence of the USA. The USA was the major power in the world and its president (Wilson) had been the driving force behind its establishment. When the USA refused to join this undermined its potential for keeping peace right from the start, because without the resources (political, economic and military) the USA could have provided, the League was unlikely to be able to respond effectively when challenged by a major power. E.g. the USA's military and economic power could have had a decisive effect in the Manchurian and Abyssinian Crises. Also, without the USA, the other major powers which were members (especially Britain and France) were more reluctant to give the League the priority and muscle it needed for success.
- However, there are other important reasons for the League's failure in the 1930s.
- The League's structure and organisation was such that it was very difficult for it to take effective action. For example, League decisions needed unanimous support and it had no effective military organisation if it was to threaten war.
- The USA was not the only major power which was not a member of the League – Germany did not join until 1926 and left in 1933, the USSR joined after Germany left. The fact that many states were not members meant that the effectiveness of economic

sanctions, for example, was severely weakened as the Abyssinian Crisis demonstrated.

- As a result of the Depression Britain and France, with their own domestic and imperial problems, were even more unwilling to take strong action on behalf of the League. What is more, as a result of the Depression, three other of the League's major powers, Japan, Italy and Germany, decided to adopt aggressive foreign policies which directly challenged the authority of the League. All three left when the League criticised their actions.
- The absence of the USA certainly weakened the League from the start. But the League failed in the 1930s not the 1920s. It was the impact of the Depression which exposed and emphasised the weaknesses of the League and brought about its failure.

2 a) Key issue: Description of key characteristics

EXAMINER'S TIP

This is a question about how? Not League aims. Focus on the means of keeping peace.

- Ideally all states would be members of the League and would agree to resolve disputes peacefully, accepting League's decisions.
- However, if a member state was attacked the League had three levels of response.
  - It could exert political pressure on the aggressor by condemning its actions.
  - It could impose economic sanctions on the aggressor (cutting off its trade).
  - It could take military action against the aggressor state.
- The basic principle was that of collective security – an attack on any one member would be regarded as an attack on them all.

b) Key issue: Explanation of a key characteristic

EXAMINER'S TIP

You need to give reasons and should deal with more than why the USA did not join.

- Some states did not join because they were not invited to, e.g. the defeated states in the First World War like Germany and Austria.
- The USSR did not join because it was distrusted by other states as it had become communist in 1917.
- The USA did not join because many in America wanted the USA to stay out of international affairs and feared being drawn into another European war. Congress voted against joining the League.

c) Key issue: Assessment of success

EXAMINER'S TIP

Plan your answer. What successes did the League have and in what areas? What failures did it have? Where does the balance lie?

- The League had success in its social and economic work. The League did tremendous work in dealing with refugees after the First World War, returning over 400 000 people to their homes. It campaigned for improved working conditions through the International Labour Organisation and some states agreed to a maximum 48-hour week. The Health Committee campaigned to reduce disease and helped in areas like leprosy and malaria. The League did much to end slavery in many parts of the world, including Sierra Leone.
- The League also had some success in resolving international disputes. In 1921 it also resolved the dispute between Sweden and Finland over the Aaland Islands in the Baltic. Perhaps its greatest success was in preventing all-out war between Greece and Bulgaria in 1925 over a border dispute. The League condemned Greek aggression which was enough to persuade it to back down.
- Throughout the 1920s the reputation of the League remained high and its membership rose. Its presence did much to help create a positive atmosphere in international relations which saw a number of international agreements designed to strengthen peace, such as the Locarno Treaties and the Kellogg-Briand Pact.
- The acid test of the League was how far it could keep peace. It resolved some disputes, but failed to resolve others. It failed to take action against Poland when its troops occupied Vilna in 1920. More significantly it acted weakly when challenged by a major power and a member state – Italy in 1923. In reaction to the killing of an Italian general on the Greek border, Mussolini of Italy bombarded and occupied the Greek island of Corfu. Greece appealed to the League which condemned Mussolini's actions. In the end, Greece was forced to apologise to Italy and pay compensation for the General's death. The League's authority had been undermined by one of its own members.
- Despite the Corfu incident, on balance, the League was successful in the 1920s. Its credibility was high, it had enjoyed success in much of its social and economic work, disputes were being resolved peacefully and no major war had broken out.

CHAPTER 5

Hitler's foreign policy

To revise this topic more thoroughly, see Chapter 5 in *Letts GCSE History Study Guide.*

 Try this sample GCSE question and then compare your answers with the Grade C and Grade A model answers pages 37 and 38.

a   Why did Hitler dislike the Treaty of Versailles?   **[4]**

b   What were Hitler's foreign policy aims?   **[6]**

c   The most **important cause** of war with Germany was Britain's policy of appeasement.

    Do you agree with this statement? Explain your answer.   **[10]**

OCR Style, Paper 1, Section B: 35 minutes

(Total 20 marks)

These two answers are at Grade C and A. Compare which one your answer is closest to and think how you could have improved it.

GRADE C ANSWER

Michael

(a) Hitler didn't like losing the war ✓ and he blamed it on the Jews. ✓ Versailles had weakened Germany. ✓

A short answer, but Michael could still score for three points made.
3/4 marks

(b) Hitler wanted all Germans to be in Germany, ✓ so he attacked Poland. He wanted to take land in eastern Europe ✓ for Germans to farm and for raw materials. ✓ He didn't want to pick a fight with Britain or France, but thought war with them would come eventually. ✓

There are several reasons here, though not well developed.
4/6 marks

(c) No, appeasement didn't cause the Second World War but Hitler did. He always intended to cause war to take over eastern Europe. ✓ He began by rearming in 1934. In 1936 he invaded the Rhineland. In 1938 he took Austria and Czechoslovakia and in 1939 he attacked Poland. ✓ Right from 1925 he was intending to attack eastwards and he promised to destroy the Treaty of Versailles ✓ in his election speeches in 1932 and 1933. He did what he said.

This does not compare appeasement with other causes of the war. There is no substance in Michael's comment about appeasement, and his information about Hitler's foreign policy is just descriptive. Above all the answer lacks balance.
5/10 marks

Grade booster ---> move a C to a B
Though these short answers score quite well, they could be considerably improved by using factual examples in more detail to explain each point.

GRADE A ANSWER

Svetlana

(a) Hitler disliked the Treaty of Versailles because he thought that Germany had not lost the war, but had been stabbed in the back by a Jewish and Communist conspiracy. ✓ The Treaty was unfair, because it was a dictated peace ('diktat') and had broken up the German nation, leaving German populations in Poland and stopping Germany uniting with Austria. ✓ The payment of reparations was hateful because it implied agreement to this dismemberment of the nation. ✓ The military restrictions were unfair because Germany could not defend or police herself. ✓

This works well because it explains why, it doesn't just repeat what Versailles did.
4/4 marks

(b) Hitler's first aim was to destroy the Treaty of Versailles and rebuild the German nation, with all Germans in one state. ✓ By 1939 he had almost achieved this, uniting Austrian and Czechoslovak Germans with Germany and destroying the military restrictions of Versailles. The war with Poland would finish this process. ✓

His second aim was 'Lebensraum', to take living space in the east at the expense of Poland, Czechoslovakia and Soviet Russia. ✓ By the end of 1939 he had taken central

This makes three main points and develops each with some fact. Each point is firmly centred on Hitler's intentions, not his actions.
6/6 marks

Hitler's foreign policy

37

Czechoslovakia and had extended his grasp of Poland far beyond the 'Polish Corridor' to create a common frontier with Soviet Russia. ✓

Hitler certainly spoke of wider aims than these: to march east to meet the Japanese Empire and take India, to beat Britain and exclude her influence from Europe, ✓ for an eventual showdown with the United States for world power, but there is no evidence that his aims were really set by 1939. He seemed to be taking opportunities as they arose rather than being certain of the future. ✓

This is a balanced answer, one half dealing with appeasement and the other looking for other causes. All through it is argued that the causes are involved with each other, to show a 'web of causation'.
9/10 marks

(c) If Britain had opposed Hitler over the remilitarisation of the Rhineland, Hitler would have backed down and little more would have been heard of him. Certainly Hitler was ready to stop the advance of German troops at the first hint of opposition, ✓ but is it likely that he would have stopped at that point and become a good citizen? Could Britain have stopped him, given that our Army was depleted and stretched throughout the Empire? ✓ Wasn't it just as much the failure of France, who had troops closer and who had insisted on the demilitarisation in the first place? The argument that appeasement was to blame ignores the fact that Britain had no other options at the time. Better to blame disarmament, ✓ the failure of the League to meet its obligations in enforcing the Treaty of Versailles, etc. Once Hitler's aggression was clear for all to see, after the invasion of Austria, Britain was forced into a miserable climbdown over Czechoslovakia, but was rearming fast so that war, avoided in the short term, could become possible later. ✓ How can a policy of avoiding, or at least postponing, war be seen as the main cause of it?

There was nothing aggressive in British policies until 1939. They were weak, but could not cause war directly. ✓ They allowed Hitler's aggression to grow, but could only have stopped him by declaring war sooner, e.g. in 1938. ✓ It was Hitler's determination to take over other countries that created the situation. He remilitarised the Rhineland in 1936, took Austria and Western Czechoslovakia in 1938, the rest of Czechoslovakia in March 1939 and then attacked Poland in September. He was the one that actually made war. ✓

A strong policy instead of appeasement was inconceivable at that time, but Hitler couldn't have continued his aggression if Britain and other nations had stood up to him earlier. ✓ That would probably still have meant war, but earlier and perhaps smaller. The failure of the League and Stalin's agreement with Hitler were probably just as important. ✓

This is one of the most important sections of the course, and everything you have learned about International Relations up to 1939 is relevant to the causes of war in 1939. Be ready to use that detail to give examples in your arguments, but remember that the argument is more important than the factual detail, which must support it.

Grade booster ····≻ move A to A*
Thorough factual knowledge will always help to boost marks from the bottom to the top of each marking level. Use factual examples constructively to prove your points.

1 Option W, International History, 1919–1963
Study Sources A and B and then answer the questions which follow.

Source A

If land was desired in Europe, it could be obtained by and large only at the expense of Russia, and this meant that the new Reich must again set itself on the march along the road of the TEUTONIC Knights of old [a medieval religious order of knighthood], to obtain by the German sword sod [earth] for the German plough and daily bread for the nation.

(extract from Hitler's Mein Kampf*)*

Source B

For this earth is not allotted to anyone … It is awarded by providence to people who in their hearts have the courage to conquer it, the strength to preserve it, and the industry to put it to the plough … Every healthy, vigorous people sees nothing sinful in territorial acquisition, but something quite in keeping with nature. The primary right of this world is the right to life, so far as one possesses the strength for this. Hence on the basis of this right a vigorous nation will always find ways of adapting its territory to its population size.

(extract from Hitler's Secret Book*, 1928)*

a) According to **Source A**, what were German foreign policy aims? ③

b) How did the League of Nations fail in Abyssinia? ⑥

c) How reliable is **Source B** to an historian writing about Hitler's foreign policy aims? ⑥

d) Were Britain and France more responsible than Hitler for the outbreak of the Second World War? Explain your answer. ⑩

AQA Style, Paper 1, Specification B: 35 minutes

TOTAL 25

---

2 a) How did the Great Depression strengthen Germany's international position? ④

b) Explain why Hitler wanted to take over Austria. ⑥

c) 'The Munich Agreement was a worthless scrap of paper.'

Do you agree with this statement? Explain your answer. ⑩

OCR Style, Paper 1, Section B: 35 minutes

TOTAL 20

Hitler's foreign policy

Hitler's foreign policy

①a) **Key issue: Comprehension of Source**

Land would be taken from Russia to gain farmland and food.

b) **Key issue: Description of key features and characteristics**

- Britain and France were more intent on preserving the Stresa Front against Germany than in protecting Abyssinia.
- Sanctions imposed in October 1935 failed, because oil was not included and non-member League nations were free to trade with Italy.
- The Hoare–Laval Pact of December 1935, was leaked and its proposers were denounced.

c) **Key issue: Evaluation of a Source for reliability in context**

- The Source was written in 1928, apparently by Hitler, so may not still represent his aims 10 years later.
- It explains Hitler's doctrine of Lebensraum – the strong taking the resources they need from the weak.
- It is corroborated both by Source A and by Hitler's actions in taking Austria, Czechoslovakia, Poland aiming to invade Russia and take the Ukraine and raw materials such as coal, iron and oil.

d) **Key issue: Explanation of causation**

- Do not limit your argument to appeasement, but show Britain and France's responsibility for the failure to maintain Versailles, the failure of the League and reduced defence spending during the Great Depression.
- Argue that causes are interconnected: Britain and France did not have the resources to deter Germany because of the Depression and their imperial commitments. Neither had the raw materials to isolate themselves from world problems, but Germany managed to do this and to spend her way out of depression quite well, partly by taking decisions which the others could not take, e.g. by exporting population and confiscating its citizens' property.
- The real reason for the war was that Hitler intended to cause war in Eastern Europe, and Britain and France fulfilled their obligations at great economic cost to themselves. If Hitler had not decided to take resources by force war would not have followed.

②a) **Key issue: Recall and description**

- While Britain and the USA concentrated resources on their home populations and reduced armaments, Germany did the reverse.
- Germany kept her population relatively poor, but created work.
- She spent money she did not have on armaments, gaining power compared to the other European powers.
- The powers in the League of Nations failed in Abyssinia because nations could not afford to impose effective sanctions.

b) **Key issue: Recall and explanation**

- Austrians are of German race and Hitler was a nationalist.
- Hitler wanted Austrian raw materials for his rearmament programme.
- Hitler was Austrian and many Austrians were Nazis and invited Germany in.

c) **Key issue: Recall, explanation and analysis**

- Hitler is said to have turned to a subordinate, after seeing Chamberlain's departure from Munich, and to have said that the Agreement was worthless. He ignored it in invading central Czechoslovakia the next March and in invading Poland.
- The Agreement delayed war, because Britain and France may have declared war to prevent a violent annexation of the Sudetenland. Hitler had now publicly given his word and would publicly break it, convincing home populations that he could not be trusted and that war was necessary. An extra year's rearmament was gained for Britain. Reluctant populations in both Britain and France realised war was inevitable in 1939.

CHAPTER 6

The Second World War 1939–1945

To revise this topic more thoroughly, see Chapter 6 in *Letts GCSE History Study Guide*.

 Try this sample GCSE question and then compare your answers with the Grade C and Grade A model answers on pages 42–44.

Study **Sources A, B, C and D** and answer all parts of the question which follow.

Source A: A painting called 'The Withdrawal from Dunkirk' by Charles Cundall. This was painted soon after the events

Source B: Statistics showing the aircraft lost by the RAF and Luftwaffe during the period July to October 1940

Date (1940)	RAF losses	Luftwaffe losses
10 July – 12 August	127	261
13 August – 6 September	385	629
7 September – 30 September	238	411
1 October – 31 October	152	297
Totals	**902**	**1598**
RAF pilots lost:	about 500	

Source C: A US army report on the D-Day landings on Omaha beach, June 1944
As the landing craft reached the beach they faced heavy shelling, machine gun and rifle fire. It came from the cliffs above the beach. Men were hit as they came down the ramps of the landing craft and as they struggled through the defences towards the land. Many others were killed by mines.

Source D: Winston Churchill comments on the importance of the Battle of the Atlantic in his book *The Second World War*

The Battle of the Atlantic was the key feature of the War. Never for one moment could we forget that everything happening elsewhere on land, sea or in the air depended on its outcome.

a   What does **Source A** tell us about the events at Dunkirk in June 1940? [3]

b   Study **Source B**. Use **Source B** and your own knowledge to explain how Britain won the Battle of Britain. [6]

c   How useful is **Source C** for explaining the difficulties facing allied troops on D-Day? Use **Source C** and your own knowledge to answer the question. [8]

d   Is **Source D** a fair interpretation of the importance of the Battle of the Atlantic to the outcome of the Second World War? Use **Source D** and your own knowledge to answer the question. [8]

(Total 25 marks)

 These two answers are at Grade C and A. Compare which one your answer is closest to and think how you could have improved it.

GRADE C ANSWER   Jessica

Just two relevant points here – troops in small boats and fighting going on. The reference to aeroplanes is not explained. This answers the question in a limited way but would still score two marks.
2/3 marks

(a) The painting tells us that many troops were taken off the beaches at Dunkirk in small boats. ✓ It also tells us that there was fighting going on during this operation because of the smoke and explosions. ✓ Aeroplanes were also involved.

This answer uses both the Source and own knowledge, but the development of the points is fairly limited.
4/6 marks

(b) This source helps explain how Britain won the Battle of Britain because it shows that the RAF shot down more German planes than it lost itself. ✓ The important part of the battle appears to be in the last two weeks of August and the first week of September when over 600 German planes were shot down. ✓ The British fighter pilots flew Spitfires and Hurricanes which were very effective planes especially against German bombers.

Jessica has commented reasonably effectively on the content and provenance (nature and origin) of the Source and gains credit for that. However, she has not used her own knowledge of the D-Day landings here.
4/8 marks

(c) This source is very useful for explaining the difficulties faced by allied troops on D-Day. The Sources tells us about the shelling, gunfire and mines and comes from a US army report about what actually happened on one of the invasion beaches. ✓ Although it may exaggerate the extent of the difficulties to make the army look good, this is a fairly reliable source from people in a position to know. ✓

A reasonable, if one-sided, answer. Jessica has commented on the Source and made use of it. She has also used some of her own knowledge. However, she has made no attempt to give an alternative interpretation of the reasons for the outcome of the war.
6/8 marks

(d) Churchill was Britain's prime minister during the war and should therefore have had a good understanding of what was important in deciding the outcome of the war. ✓ He believes winning the Battle of the Atlantic was the key to success. Certainly Britain depended on supplies coming in across and through the Atlantic to keep her fed and bring war supplies, so defeating the U-boats was very important. ✓ Despite U-boats sinking thousands of ships the supply routes were kept open. ✓ This allowed the USA to bring her army to Europe and help us win the war. Churchill's interpretation is fair, therefore. ✓

Grade booster ···> move a C to a B

To score more highly, Jessica needs to make more use of her own knowledge. She also needs to develop her explanations more fully. In the essay question she needs to provide a more balanced answer.

Anil

(a) This painting, from the time, shows us the way the troops were evacuated from the beaches at Dunkirk. ✓ You can see the variety of small boats and merchant ships being used alongside Royal Navy ships. You can also see the pressure the British army was under. The billowing smoke and explosions from shells, with the aerial fighting going on shows that this was an evacuation taking place in the midst of battle. ✓ The painting illustrates what a remarkable achievement it was to evacuate so many thousands of British troops when they were being attacked by the German forces. ✓

A good answer which uses the details of the painting to good effect. Anil has also drawn an overall conclusion about the evacuation from the information in the painting.
3/3 marks

(b) In July 1940 Hitler aimed to destroy the British air force as a prelude to the invasion of Britain in Operation Sealion. Although the statistics in Source B go beyond the events of July, August and early September and into the Blitz, they clearly illustrate the pressure the RAF was under and the success the RAF had in destroying German aircraft. ✓ The RAF losses were in fighter aircraft, whilst most of the German losses were bombers. This helps to explain the differences in the figures. ✓ Clearly, preventing the Luftwaffe from gaining air superiority was crucial in defeating Hitler's plans to invade Britain. This the RAF did, with the main effort being made in the last two weeks of August and the beginning of September. The cost was high, though, as the statistics relating to the loss of pilots indicate. ✓ Fortunately, the RAF had done enough by mid-September to stop the invasion and the Germans changed their tactics to bombing British cities (the Blitz) rather than the airfields.

This full answer shows a good understanding of the Battle of Britain and the role played by the RAF. Use is made of the statistics to support the points made.
6/6 marks

(c) Source C is very useful in explaining the difficulties faced by allied troops in the D-Day landings. It clearly highlights the problems faced — heavy shelling, machine gun and rifle fire, and mines. ✓ The landings were resisted. Its usefulness is enhanced by the fact that it comes from a reliable source — a US army report on the landings written at the time (June 1944). ✓ Whilst one might suspect that there could be some exaggeration of the degree of resistance in order to make the efforts of the US army look more impressive, there is no reason to disbelieve the essence of the account. However, this source does only refer to one of the landing beaches and the difficulties faced by allied troops on other beaches

This answer deals with the usefulness in terms of its content and its nature, origin and purpose. It also, crucially, recognises not just the strengths but also the limitations of the Source by reference to relevant historical knowledge. This ensures a high mark.
7/8 marks

The Second World War 1939–1945

were less. ✓ On Omaha beach the US army met with far greater resistance than on Utah beach or that the British and Canadians met on Gold, Juno and Sword. ✓

(d) The Battle of the Atlantic refers to the struggle to deal with the U-boat threat in the Atlantic which endangered Britain's sea routes. It was vital that these be kept open not only for war supplies but also for food. ✓ In 1939 Britain only produced enough food to feed one in three of the population. From the very start of the war the Germans had decided to attack this vital area. Admiral Doenitz agreed with Churchill that Britain's ability to maintain her supply lines was vital to her war effort. ✓ During the war German U-boats sank nearly 3000 ships, despite the use of convoys and other systems of defence. By 1943, however, the tide began to turn in Britain's favour as more warships were deployed and aircraft and code-breaking meant the detection of U-boats became more effective. Clearly, Churchill was right in that the actions of the U-boats, at least up until 1942, had the potential to strangle Britain's war effort. ✓ Churchill, as wartime prime minister, was also in a good position to judge the importance of keeping open Britain's sea routes. It was vital to Britain's survival. It was also vital to make the Atlantic secure if the USA was to be able to wage war effectively in Europe. Whether the Battle of the Atlantic was vital to the outcome of the Second World War is, however, more debatable. Many would argue that the resistance of Russia was at least as important as the Battle of the Atlantic. ✓ Some might also argue that if Britain had not won the Battle of Britain the outcome of the war may have been very different. ✓

This sound answer shows a good knowledge and understanding of the Battle of the Atlantic and its role in the war. Anil also uses the Source quite effectively, referring to the German's view that the Battle of the Atlantic was crucial. There is also some evaluation of the Source. Churchill's interpretation is also set in the context of wider historical knowledge and the role of other factors in the outcome of the war.

7/8 marks

Grade booster ····▷ move A to A*

Anil's answer to c could be sharpened up by emphasising the factual nature of the account – the language and tone of the piece are sober and straightforward. In his answer to d he could make direct reference to Source D and comment directly on it as an interpretation.

1 This question is about Operation Barbarossa, the German invasion of the Soviet Union in 1941. Look carefully at **Sources A to F** and then answer the questions a) to d) which follow.

Source A: A map showing the German invasion of the Soviet Union

Source B: From a school textbook about the history of the Soviet Union in the twentieth century, published in Britain in 1991

The Nazi–Soviet pact was fragile and likely to break down when it suited either of the parties. There is no evidence that Stalin was preparing a war against Germany. It seems more likely that Hitler's long term hatred of Bolshevism and wish to gain Lebensraum (living space) played the key role in his decision to attack the Soviet Union.

Source C: From a book about international relations, published in Britain in 1997

On 22 June 1941, Germany made a surprise attack on the Soviet Union. Operation Barbarossa was a three-pronged attack on the cities of Leningrad, Moscow and Stalingrad. The plan would lead to the destruction of the Soviet Union and would give Germany access to wheatfields of the Ukraine and the oilfields of the Caucasus. Germany would also gain living space.

Source D: From the diary of General Halder, August 1941. Halder was one of the German commanders leading the German invasion

We have underestimated the Russian giant. At the start of the war, we reckoned we would face about 200 enemy divisions. Now we have already counted about 360. Time favours the Russians. They are near their own resources and we are moving further away from ours. Our troops are spread out over an immense line and are subjected to the enemy's constant attacks.

Source E: Photograph showing Soviet troops in action against the Germans in 1941

Source F: From Stalin's radio broadcast to the Soviet people at the time of the German invasion, June 1941

The enemy is cruel. They are out to seize our lands, our grain, our oil. They are out to restore the role of landlords, to turn our people into the slaves of Germany. If we are forced to retreat, the enemy must not be left a single engine, a single pound of grain or a gallon of fuel. All valuable property including grain and fuel that cannot be withdrawn must be destroyed without fail. In areas occupied by the enemy, guerrillas must be formed, sabotage groups must be organised to combat the enemy by blowing up bridges and roads.

a) Study **Source A**. What can you learn from this source about the aims of the German invasion of the Soviet Union? ④

b) Study **Sources A, B and C**. Does **Source C** support the evidence of **Sources A and B**? Explain your answer. ⑥

c) Study **Sources D and E**. How useful are these two sources as evidence about the problems faced by the German armies in the Soviet Union? ⑧

d) Study all the Sources. 'Operation Barbarossa failed because it was badly planned.' Use the sources, and your own knowledge, to explain whether you agree with this view. ⑫

Edexcel Style, Paper 2: 50 minutes

TOTAL 30

a) **Key issue: Understanding of the Source**

EXAMINER'S TIP

Be brief and make three clear points.

- To capture the Ukrainian wheatfields
- To capture the oilfields of the Caucasus
- To destroy the USSR.

b) **Key issue: Corroboration by cross-referencing between Sources**

EXAMINER'S TIP

Look for areas of support and lack of support. Refer to all the Sources.

- Source C supports Source A – it talks of a three-pronged attack towards Leningrad, Moscow and Stalingrad. It also talks of capturing the Ukrainian wheatfields and the Caucasian oilfields.
- Source C supports Source B – it refers to the gaining of 'living space' (Lebensraum) and implies the destruction of the Soviet Union by referring to Hitler's hatred of Bolshevism.
- There is no mention of a surprise attack in A or B, nor is there direct support in C for the idea that the Nazi–Soviet Pact was fragile and likely to break down.

c) **Key issue: Evaluation of Sources for usefulness**

EXAMINER'S TIP

Aim to refer not just to content but also the nature of the Sources.

- Source D suggests the Russian army was much larger than anticipated and points out the disadvantages of distance from supplies the Germans face. In it General Halder also is concerned about the constant attacks of the Russians and the way the German troops are spread over a wide area.
- This source is useful because it written by a senior German officer who would be in a position to comment authoritatively. It is also a diary entry and so probably gives the General's honest appraisal of the situation.
- The Source expresses the General's fears and gives no positive side to the German position. It is therefore a little one-sided.
- Source E shows well-equipped Russian troops which to some extent confirms Halder's fears about constant Russian attacks. It also shows the Russian winter for which the Russian troops were well-prepared (for example, the white camouflage the troops are wearing). In

contrast the German army was not well-prepared for a winter campaign.
- It would be dangerous to draw too strong conclusions from a single photograph – may not have been typical of all Russian troops.

d) **Key issue: Making a judgement about an interpretation based on Sources and contextual knowledge**

EXAMINER'S TIP

Plan your answer, organising evidence for and against the given assessment. This will enable you to come to a balanced conclusion.

- There is certainly evidence in the sources that the Operation was not planned well. Source D especially suggests that the Germans miscalculated the size of the Russian army and the scale of the operation. Sources A and C also show that the operation had a number of different aims which helped to compound the problems indicated in D.
- The German attack did not take place until June 1941, which shortened the period for success to be achieved before the Russian winter brought the German advances to a halt.
- However, the Germans achieved spectacular advances in the summer of 1941, but as Source D indicates, the length of their advance worked against the Germans who found themselves further and further away from their sources of supply.
- Bad planning was not the only reason for the failure of Operation Barbarossa. Stalin had ordered a scorched earth policy as the Russians retreated (Source F), leaving nothing for the German army to use. Partisans were also active behind the front lines harrying communications (also ordered by Stalin in Source F). In this way the Russians made effective use of the great distances the Germans had to keep open supply lines. As they advanced, troops had to be left to guard supply posts and communications, weakening the attacking forces. As Halder (Source D) indicated as early as August the German troops were increasingly thinly spread.
- More than anything perhaps, it was the onset of the Russian winter that brought Operation Barbarossa to a halt (Source E). German tanks could not operate in the sub-zero temperatures and the German army was ill-equipped to fight a winter war. The Russians meanwhile dug-in and had better-equipped troops for winter warfare (Source E).

CHAPTER 7

The causes of the Cold War

To revise this topic more thoroughly, see Chapter 7 in *Letts GCSE History Study Guide*.

 Try this sample GCSE question and then compare your answers with the Grade C and Grade A model answers on pages 49 and 50.

Study **Source A** and answer all parts of the question which follow.

Source A: A Soviet view of the Marshall Plan

The Americans said that the Marshall Plan was 'a plan to save peace'. This was not true. It was really intended to unite countries against the Soviet Union.

The Marshall Plan of 1947 led to a reduction in the trade of the Soviet Union and the other communist countries with the rest of the world. The USA hoped that this would lead to a split among the communist states and bring them under American influence. It was also clear that much of the Marshall Plan was aimed at rebuilding the military power of Western Germany.

(from Soviet Foreign Policy, *by I.S. Kremer, 1968)*

a According to **Source A**, why did the Americans introduce the Marshall Plan? [3]
b How reliable is the view of the Marshall Plan given in **Source A**? [6]
c Describe how Stalin tried to take over Berlin and was prevented by the West in 1948–9. [6]
d Why did the rivalry between the USA and the USSR increase in the period 1945–1955? Explain your answer. [10]

AQA, Paper 1 (Specimen Paper) Option X pages 12 and 20

(Total 25 marks)

These two answers are at Grade C and A. Compare which one your answer is closest to and think how you could have improved it.

GRADE C ANSWER

Jonathan

(a) To stop communism from spreading into Europe. ✓

(b) The Source says that the Russians thought that the Americans wanted to take over Europe, ✓ whereas I know that it was the Russians that were taking the whole of Eastern Europe for themselves. ✓

(c) When Stalin had taken over the rest of Eastern Europe, only West Berlin remained in British, French and American hands. ✓ Stalin decided to get us out of there by cutting off all links and letting Berlin starve. ✓ The West couldn't allow this, so they organised an airlift to take food and fuel in. ✓ This was a terrific success, with planes taking off and landing every 30 seconds. ✓ So Stalin was outwitted and West Berlin remained free.

(d) At the end of the Second World War, Stalin was given Eastern Europe as his 'sphere of influence' but he was expected to make sure that free elections were held in each state. ✓ He didn't, and communist governments spread through Eastern Europe so rapidly that, by 1946, Winston Churchill spoke of an 'iron curtain'✓ and so the Americans began the Marshall Plan. ✓ In 1948 there was the Berlin Airlift ✓ and the USA began NATO in 1949. ✓

Jonathan must use the Source! Even so, he has made one markable point.
1/3 marks

He uses his own knowledge to compare with the Source and makes a simple point. If he had described bias, he would have improved this answer.
3/6 marks

This answer works quite well. It gives the essential story, but needed some of the points to be developed to gain top marks.
4/6 marks

This is a narrative, not a direct answer giving reasons. Events are given correctly, in their correct order, but without explanation. Concentrate on a few reasons, properly explained.
5/10 marks

> ### Grade booster ⋯⟩ move a C to a B
> Jonathan must develop his answers in more detail and write more on each answer. Think carefully about each task. Some say 'describe' and others ask 'why?' You must do as they ask. Don't write the same kind of answer for every question.

GRADE A ANSWER

Nicole

a) The plan was 'intended to unite countries against the Soviet Union'. ✓ The plan 'led to a reduction in the trade of the Soviet Union and the other communist countries with the rest of the world.' ✓ 'The USA hoped that this would lead to a split among the communist states and bring them under American influence.' ✓ 'The Marshall Plan was aimed at rebuilding the military power of Western Germany.' ✓

b) The Soviet source was written in 1968, fully twenty years after the event, ✓ so might not reflect the actual feelings of 1947, but of the year of the invasion of Czechoslovakia. ✓

The Soviet version leaves out everything that they had done to alarm the West, ✓ such as the destruction of democracy behind the 'Iron Curtain'.✓

The Marshall Plan was intended to, and did, stop the slide towards socialism in Western Europe. ✓ It was particularly important in shoring up the economy of West Germany, both points covered to some degree in this extract. ✓

c) The Western Powers wanted West Germany to recover quickly, had included it in the Marshall Plan and it's economy was recovering fast. The USSR wanted to keep West Germany weak. ✓

In 1948 the Deutschmark was introduced into Western Germany and Western sectors of Berlin. This annoyed Stalin, who accused the West of interfering in Eastern Germany (because Berlin was in the East). ✓

Russia closed off all road, rail and water communication with West Berlin, leaving only two air corridors open. Berlin could not feed itself, so Britain, France and the USA had to find a way to keep it supplied, or give in. War with a superior Russian army could not be contemplated. ✓

The solution, to supply Berlin by air, left it to the Russians to start a war or back down. ✓

The blockade lasted nearly a year until the Russians lifted it in May 1949. ✓ It made the West Berliners even more determined not to become East German, and was the first Western victory against the encroachment of Communism. It prompted the founding of NATO. ✓

d) USSR was a communist country and had always suspected the capitalist USA and vice versa. ✓

While the Yalta Conference had allowed Eastern Europe to become part of the Soviet 'sphere of influence' it also said that there should be free elections, which there were not. ✓ America was worried that the USSR was spreading Communism across Europe, ✓ and about the huge number of Soviet troops stationed just beyond the Iron Curtain. ✓

The Marshall Plan and the Atom Bomb both seemed to the USSR to be aggressive moves against them by the USA. ✓

Everyone mistrusted everyone else. ✓

Grade booster ⋯⋯⟩ move A to A*

To improve, Nicole needs to mention some events, and the ways that they increased tension, e.g. the Berlin Blockade. An appreciation of exactly how little needs to be written to gain each mark is essential. A really good candidate should be aware of shortness of time and move on after each mark is scored.

QUESTION BANK

1 The photograph shows the leaders of the Allies at Potsdam in 1945. Study the photograph and then answer all the questions that follow.

a) Give **ONE** reason to explain why the Allies met at Potsdam in 1945. ③

b) Describe the key features of the Truman Doctrine, 1947. ⑤

c) Why was NATO formed in 1949? ⑤

d) Why did North Korea fail to conquer the South by 1953? ⑦

Edexcel A Style Question: 30 minutes

TOTAL 20

---

2 a) What did the Allies agree at the Yalta Conference? ④

b) Why did Churchill make his famous 'iron curtain' speech in 1946? ⑥

c) 'The Cold War was inevitable because both the USA and Soviet Russia threatened each other by their political views.' Do you agree with this statement? Explain your answer. ⑩

OCR B Style Question, Paper 1: 35 minutes

TOTAL 20

---

3 **Source A: A British view of the Soviet threat**
From Stettin in the Baltic, to Trieste, in the Adriatic, an iron curtain has descended across the continent. Behind that curtain ... all are subject to Soviet influence and a very high measure of control from Moscow.

(Winston Churchill March 1946)

a) According to **Source A**, what was the 'Iron Curtain'? ③

b) How reliable is the view of the reasons for Cold War given in **Source A**? ⑥

c) Describe how the Western Powers reacted to this threat between 1947 and 1949. ⑥

d) Why did the Berlin Crisis of 1948–9 not result in open warfare between the West and the Soviet Union? ⑩

AQA Style Question, Paper 1: 35 minutes

TOTAL 25

The causes of the Cold War

1 a) **Key issue: Understanding of key feature/recall of knowledge**

EXAMINER'S TIP

Give a simple reason, then explain it.

- They met to discuss the future of Germany. Stalin had taken control of Eastern Europe, and wanted Germany to remain weak. Truman didn't want to repeat the mistakes of Versailles and wanted to treat Germany well.

b) **Key issue: Causation/recall of knowledge**

EXAMINER'S TIP

Each key point needs to be accompanied by some explanation of why it mattered.

- The United States came back out of isolation to prevent the spread of communism.
- Truman promised to protect 'free people', i.e. democracy and anti-communist states.
- Truman would protect them against 'armed minorities or outside pressures', meaning communist take-overs and the USSR.
- This promise held good for anywhere in the world, whether or not American interests were directly threatened.

c) **Key issue: Key features/recall of knowledge**

EXAMINER'S TIP

You need to develop each reason to show how it was linked to the others.

- Even during the war the USA and the USSR had been suspicious of each other because of their different ideologies.
- After the Yalta Conference Soviet Russia denied the states within its 'sphere of influence' in Eastern Europe the right to democracy and stationed huge numbers of troops there threatening the West.
- Once Churchill had pointed out the situation, Truman consolidated US influence, both by the Marshall Plan and by the Truman Doctrine. This created a confrontational situation, close to war.
- In 1948 the Berlin Crisis almost caused the war, but the USA did not have enough troops in Europe to take on the Soviet Union, and the Russians were scared of the American Atomic Bomb (which they could

not yet match). So the Berlin Airlift was allowed to succeed without open warfare. By 1949 both superpowers wanted to consolidate their power: the West set up NATO, the USSR exploded their first atomic bomb.

d) **Key issue: Causation/analysis of consequence/recall of knowledge**

EXAMINER'S TIP

Again, show the links between the causes you give and give some detail for each one.

- The Communist North Koreans were supported by Soviet Russia. In 1950 they nearly succeeded in taking South Korea, being held up only at the Pusan Perimeter.
- US troops had gone to support the South Koreans as soon as they were attacked. General MacArthur counter-attacked at Inchon, taking the North Koreans in the rear. Armed with a UN mandate, he attacked the North so successfully that UN troops approached the Yalu River border with China. At this point Chinese 'volunteers' poured over the border in support of communist North Korea.
- The Chinese troops helped the North Koreans to push the United Nations back. MacArthur wanted to use the Atomic Bomb but was removed by Truman. Eventually the front was stabilised at the 38th parallel, not far from the original North/South border. An armistice was signed in 1953.

2 a) **Key issue: Recall, select, organise and deploy knowledge**

EXAMINER'S TIP

Either give four quick points, or two developed points.

- German forces were to be demobilised and war criminals punished.
- Germany would be divided between USSR, USA, France, Britain.
- The United Nations was set up.
- Eastern Europe became Soviet.

b) **Key issue: Recall, select, organise and deploy knowledge**

EXAMINER'S TIP

Give reasons, but explain them too to double the marks.

- The alliance between the USA and Britain had lapsed, Britain was bankrupt and could not fulfil her international obligations without US help.
- The USA seemed to be moving back into isolation just at the stage when the Soviet threat to Europe was growing.
- The USSR was extending its influence denying Eastern Europe countries free elections.

c) **Key issue: Recall, select, organise and deploy knowledge**

EXAMINER'S TIP

Show a variety of different reasons, but also show how they interrelate.

- Communism and capitalism are opposite views about politics and economics, and one seemed to threaten the other.
- There are many other explanations for the Cold War, such as the personal suspicion between Stalin and Truman, the fear in the Soviet Union of invasion by Western powers, (twice in the previous 30 years), the imbalance of the nuclear arms race while the USSR did not have the A bomb, the pressure of events, such as the Greek emergency and the Berlin crisis, both of which made the situation worse.
- All these reasons are interconnected because mutual suspicion and the growth of rivalry provoked events, each of which made the situation worse.

❸ a) **Key issue: Comprehension of Source**

EXAMINER'S TIP

Make three good points, using the Source.

- A border stretching from the Baltic to the Adriatic.
- Behind that border 'all are subject to Soviet influence', – they had lost their rights to democracy.
- 'A very high measure of control from Moscow' – the Soviet Union has dictatorial powers and these states have lost their independence.

b) **Key issue: Evaluation of a source for reliability**

EXAMINER'S TIP

Who wrote (said) it and why? What are its strengths and limitations in answering the question?

- Unreliable because it is dated so early that the later reasons for the development of the Cold War cannot be included.
- Churchill wanted to shock his American audience into believing that the resumption of US influence in Europe was essential.
- Both the tone and the content show the alarm of many at the huge extension of Soviet power.

c) **Key issue: Description of key features and characteristics**

EXAMINER'S TIP

You need to give a detailed description of several aspects of the reaction of the West.

- In 1947 the USA began the Marshall Plan, which correctly analysed communism in Western Europe as being caused by poverty, and began to put this right by huge financial aid from the USA. In the same year, President Truman promised help to all free people and committing the USA to opposing the further extension of Soviet influence. These two measures had consolidated the US position, both in Europe and elsewhere.
- The two superpowers were ranged against each other, and in 1948 conflict nearly erupted in the Berlin Crisis. The USA avoided a direct confrontation through the Airlift, but the Crisis worsened the situation.
- In 1949 the USA constructed the NATO to unite the West and to show the determination to resist further encroachment in Berlin or anywhere else.

d) **Key issue: Explanation of causation**

EXAMINER'S TIP

You need a relevant, thorough, multicausal answer here.

- The Second World War was lately over, countries were reluctant to fight and the conflict between communism and the West would have been so serious that no one would willingly start it.
- Neither the Soviet Union, in cutting off food supplies, nor the USA in starting the Airlift, was doing enough to provoke open warfare. The fear was that each side might be mistaken in judging how far they could.
- Both powers were at a disadvantage, the USA because they did not have enough troops on the ground to resist the Soviet army, the USSR because it did not yet have its own atom bomb.
- So neither side could afford to seem the aggressor, without causing a catastrophe.

The causes of the Cold War

CHAPTER 8

Tension and détente 1950–1991

To revise this topic more thoroughly, see Chapter 8 in *Letts GCSE History Study Guide.*

 Try this sample GCSE question and then compare your answers with the Grade C and Grade A model answers on pages 55 and 56.

a Describe the military tactics of the Vietcong. **[4]**

b Why did the Americans get involved in Vietnam? **[6]**

c 'The most important reason for American defeat was their failure to win support from the Vietnamese peasants.' Do you agree with this statement? Explain your answer. **[10]**

OCR Style Paper 1 question: 35 minutes

(Total 20 marks)

These two answers are at Grade C and A. Compare which one your answer is closest to and think how you could have improved it.

GRADE C ANSWER

Naomi

(a) The Viet Cong were communists who fought using guerrilla tactics, like attacking buildings and government officials. ✓

(b) The Americans got involved in Vietnam because they didn't want it to become communist. ✓ They thought that if Vietnam became communist then other countries in Southern Asia would as well. ✓

(c) The failure to win the support of the Vietnamese peasants was certainly very important in explaining America's defeat in Vietnam, but there are a number of other reasons.

They were fighting a strong and determined enemy that adopted clever tactics for fighting the numerically and technically stronger US and South Vietnamese forces. The Viet Cong were expert guerrilla fighters who were strong believers in the communist cause. ✓ They were difficult to fight because the Americans found them difficult to spot amongst the peasants.

American troops often had low morale and were inexperienced. ✓ The average age of the US soldier was 19 and he was fighting in a foreign country thousands of miles away from home.

American tactics did not work. ✓ Bombing of the Ho Chi Minh trail upon which the Viet Cong depended did not close it. 'Search and destroy' missions against Vietnamese villages often killed more civilians than Viet Cong.

The American public turned against the war. Vietnam was on television and radio and news reporters brought information about the war into every American home. Many people turned against the war which was very expensive and was costing many young American lives. ✓ News of massacres like that at My Lai made many believe America should get out of a war they could not win. There were mass protests against the war. So there are a number of reasons why the Americans were defeated.

Naomi has made the essential point that the Viet Cong used guerrilla tactics and has made a limited attempt to describe the kind of things this involved.
2/4 marks

Naomi has got the essence of a good answer here. She has recognised the US's fears of communism spreading. However, she needs to develop this answer a little bit more.
4/6 marks

Naomi has dealt with a number of factors involved in explaining America's defeat. In many ways she has handled these well, explaining them with supporting detail. The great weakness of the answer is, however, that she does not really deal with the factor raised in the question – the failure to win the support of the peasants. If she had explained this factor and drawn a conclusion explaining why she considered one or more reasons were more important than others, she could easily get into the top bands.
6/10 marks

Grade booster ···⟩ move a C to a B
Read the exam question carefully, make sure you really have answered what you have been asked and support your answer with a good use of detail. Where an essay question asks you about the relative importance of one factor, it is very important you explain why **that** factor is important before you consider the other factors.

GRADE A ANSWER

Jacob

A full and intelligent answer, showing a sound appreciation of guerrilla tactics and what the Viet Cong hoped to achieve by them.
4/4 marks

(a) The Viet Cong were expert guerrilla fighters. ✓ They were indistinguishable from Vietnamese peasants, ✓ mounted attacks on government buildings and officials, ambushed patrolling soldiers and then melted away into the countryside. ✓ They were kept supplied down the Ho Chi Minh trail. ✓ By working with the peasants they made much of the countryside unsafe for government forces. They avoided open battle with South Vietnamese or US forces but instead aimed to wear down enemy soldiers and break their morale. ✓

A good quality answer which gives similar reasons to Naomi's above, but develops and explains them more carefully.
6/6 marks

(b) The basic reason why the Americans got involved in Vietnam was their desire to contain the spread of communism. ✓ That is why they supported the corrupt anti-communist government of Diem, first financially and then militarily. ✓ Americans were convinced that the USSR and China wanted to spread communism around the world. ✓ They feared that if Vietnam went communist then Laos, Cambodia, Thailand, Burma and even India would follow. ✓ This they called the domino effect. ✓

An effective answer covering four major factors in American defeat. Crucially Jacob has carefully considered the role of the Vietnamese peasantry and linked that to other factors.
8/10 marks

(c) The failure to win the support of the peasants was a vital reason in explaining America's defeat in Vietnam. If the Americans had won the support of the peasants the Viet Cong would have found it very difficult to operate in South Vietnam where they relied on being able to melt into the countryside. ✓ In contrast to the Americans the Viet Cong made great efforts to win over the peasants by being courteous and polite and helping in the fields. ✓ In contrast, American tactics tended to increase peasant hostility to armed forces they already regarded as foreign invaders. American 'search and destroy' missions led to the killing of innocent Vietnamese, most notably at My Lai in 1968. ✓ American bombing also led to civilian deaths and the use of 'Agent Orange' and napalm also caused many deaths. ✓

But the lack of peasant support was not the only reason for American defeat. Clearly the quality and tactics of their enemy, the Viet Cong, supported from North Vietnam down the Ho Chi Minh trail, were very important. ✓ They won over the peasants, were determined fighters, used effective guerrilla tactics and never gave in. They could even surprise the US army by mounting a huge and unexpected attack in the Tet Offensive in 1968. ✓

America's war effort was also undermined from home. ✓ In a democracy, war requires public support and in the late 1960s public opinion in the USA became highly critical of the war as it became clearer that the war could not be won. Mass protest marches took place and news of atrocities like My Lai undermined the military.

Finally in contrast to the Viet Cong, the quality of American forces was not always high. Most troops were young and inexperienced and fighting against an unseen enemy thousands of miles from home. ✓

Grade booster ····▷ move A to A*
In his final answer Jacob could have explained a little more fully how the factors linked together and why one was more important and others were less important.

① Study **Sources A and B** and then answer the questions which follow.

Source A: A British cartoon about the struggle between the leaders of the USSR and USA over the Cuban Missile Crisis

Source B: The Russian leader explains his view of the outcome of the missile crisis in *Khrushchev Remembers*, published in 1971

We agreed to remove our missiles and bombers on condition that the President promised that there would be no invasion of Cuba by the forces of the United States or anybody else. Finally Kennedy gave in and agreed. It was a great victory for us, a spectacular success without having to fire a single shot.

a) According to **Source A,** what was the Cuban Missile Crisis about?   ③

b) Describe how the Cuban Missile Crisis came about.   ⑥

c) How accurate is Khrushchev's view of the results of the Cuban Missile Crisis as stated in **Source B**? Use **Source B** and your own knowledge to answer the question.   ⑥

d) How far did relations between the USSR and the USA improve between 1962 and 1991?   ⑩

AQA Style Paper 1, Section A Question: 35 minutes

TOTAL 25

2 You must answer Part a) and Part b) of this question.

a) Part a) of this question is about détente after 1963. The photograph below shows President Gorbachev and President Reagan. Look at the photograph and then answer all the questions which follow.

i) What was meant by 'peaceful coexistence'? ③

ii) Describe the key features of the Strategic Arms Limitation Talks (SALT I and SALT II). ⑤

iii) Why did relations between the USA and the USSR worsen following the Soviet invasion of Afghanistan? ⑤

iv) In what ways did President Gorbachev attempt to end the Cold War? ⑦

b) Part b) of this question is about the development of the Cold War between 1953 and 1962.

i) Describe how relations between the USA and the USSR changed in the years 1953 to 1961. ⑩

You may use the following information to help you with your answer.
1953 Death of Stalin
1955 Warsaw Pact
1956 Hungarian Uprising
1957 Sputnik
1961 Berlin Wall

ii) Why was there such a major crisis between the Superpowers over Cuba in 1962? ⑩

Edexcel Style question: 60 minutes

TOTAL 40

① a) Key issue: Understanding of Source

EXAMINER'S TIP

Look carefully at the details of the cartoon to make sure you understand the message. Your answer can be short and to the point.

- Source A suggests that the Cuban Missile Crisis was a test of strength between the two Superpowers, each trying to make the other back down.
- It was a struggle which threatened to produce a nuclear war (both leaders are sitting on nuclear missiles and are threatening to press the nuclear button).

b) Key issue: Description of a key event

EXAMINER'S TIP

Keep to the main aspects of the origins of the Crisis and make sure you use accurate details.

- In 1959 Castro overthrew the American supported ruler of Cuba, Batista. America then refused to trade with Cuba which turned to the USSR for help.
- The USSR agreed to buy Cuban sugar. This angered America and President Kennedy agreed to an attempt to overthrow Castro which resulted in failure in the 'Bay of Pigs' in 1961.
- Castro now declared himself a communist and the USSR sent military aid, including medium-range nuclear missiles in September.
- Such missiles represented a direct threat to the security of the USA and Kennedy demanded their withdrawal and blockaded Cuba.
- On 24 October Soviet ships carrying more nuclear missiles approached the blockade. The Cuban Missile Crisis had begun. Both sides now had to consider how far they would be willing to go.

c) Key issue: Use of Source and own knowledge to assess validity of an interpretation

EXAMINER'S TIP

Make sure you use both the Source and your own knowledge in answering this question. Do not forget to take account of the nature, origin and purpose of the Source in making your assessment.

- Source B is accurate in so far as the USSR did agree to remove its missiles and bombers and the USA did leave Cuba alone.
- Khrushchev was certainly in a good position to judge the outcome of the Crisis, being one of the two leaders involved. However, Khrushchev is only giving part of the answer here. He wants to portray the outcome of the Crisis as a success for the Soviet Union as he was Soviet leader at that time and he is perhaps defending himself in his memoirs.
- America would argue that it was a success for President Kennedy because the Soviets were forced to remove their missiles whilst the Americans did not agree to remove missiles from Turkey. Certainly it removed the direct nuclear threat from a near neighbour of the USA.
- For the rest of the world, however, the major result of the Crisis was perhaps that nuclear war had not occurred – both sides in the end had drawn back from the brink.
- Overall, therefore Source B is only partially accurate in its verdict on the results. It was certainly not really a success for the USSR.

d) Key issue: Evaluation of a historical development

EXAMINER'S TIP

The questions asks 'How far?' This means you are expected to consider evidence both for and against the idea of improvement and come to a balanced judgement. Plan your answer before writing it!

- There is some evidence that relations did improve after 1962. A hotline was established between Washington and Moscow in June 1963 so that matters of difference between the Superpowers could be discussed before a crisis emerged. There was also some attempt to contain or control the proliferation of nuclear weapons. Both the USA and the USSR signed up to the Nuclear Test Ban Treaty in August 1963 and in 1968 there came the Nuclear Non-Proliferation Treaty. In the 1970s there was also a period of 'Détente' (relaxation of tension) between the Superpowers resulting in the SALT agreements to limit nuclear weapons, the Helsinki Agreement (1975) on human rights and agreement to borders, and a variety of cultural and sporting exchanges and visits, including summits between Soviet and US leaders. With the coming to power of Gorbachev in the USSR relations improved again as the Soviet leader introduced policies of Glasnost and Perestroika, leading to the INF treaty (December 1987).

- However, relations between the superpowers were often difficult and frosty. The Vietnam war (which involved both powers) created tension as did the Soviet invasion of Czechoslovakia (1968). Then in the 1980s the Afghan war and President Reagan's SDI (Star Wars) initiative caused tensions.
- Overall, relations did improve, but the development of improved relations was not steady nor did it result in open trust, even after the collapse of the Soviet Union.

❷a) i) Key issue: Understanding of a key feature

EXAMINER'S TIP

You need to give a brief explanation of the term in its historical context.

- The idea of 'peaceful coexistence' was put forward by Khrushchev, the Russian leader, in 1956. It signalled a desire to move away from the Cold War and hostile stance of his predecessor Stalin.
- By it he meant the idea that capitalism (USA) and communism (USSR) could live together in the world by a policy of mutual toleration.

ii) Key issue: Knowledge of key features/events

EXAMINER'S TIP

You need to show you know the key features of what was agreed in both SALT I and SALT II.

- The Strategic Arms Limitation Talks were a significant result of the process of Détente in the 1970s. They were concerned with the limitation of nuclear weapons held by both the USA and the USSR.
- In SALT I (1972) both sides agreed to reduce their anti-ballistic missile systems and to limit the number of their nuclear missiles and bombers.
- In SALT II (1979) there was more tension, but an agreement was reached to further limit nuclear weapons.
- However, in 1980 President Carter of the USA refused to agree the SALT II treaty because of the Soviet invasion of Afghanistan.
- In the 1980s, the SALT negotiations were replaced in 1982 by the Strategic Arms Reduction Talks (START).

iii) Key issue: Understanding of causation

EXAMINER'S TIP

To score highly you will need to identify reasons and support them with appropriate knowledge.

- The invasion worsened relations because Afghanistan was important strategically for the USA as well as the USSR, being close to the Middle East oilfields. Both sides had been trying to increase their influence.
- President Carter called the invasion a threat to world peace and relations deteriorated further when he decided not to ratify SALT II, to impose trade sanctions and to boycott the Moscow Olympics (1980). He also sent extra forces to the Middle East. In 1984 the USSR boycotted the Los Angeles Olympics.
- Effectively the Soviet invasion put an end to Détente and started a second 'cold war'. The USA declared they were ready to act if the USSR moved beyond Afghanistan.

iv) Key issue: Understanding of key features

EXAMINER'S TIP

You need to identify several ways in which Gorbachev acted to reduce East–West tension and support them with relevant detail.

- Gorbachev became Soviet leader in 1985 and immediately set about taking actions which eased tensions.
- He worked to withdraw Soviet troops from Afghanistan.
- He was willing and anxious to reduce military expenditure which opened the way for arms talks with the USA to resume – the result was the INF treaty of 1987.
- His policies of Glasnost and Perestroika were welcomed in the West as steps towards democracy.
- He ended the Brezhnev Doctrine in Eastern Europe in 1989, ending the threat of Soviet intervention and Soviet troops were withdrawn.
- He encouraged Western investment in the Soviet Union.
- Most significantly perhaps he met several times with President Reagan of the USA. He believed Gorbachev was a man he could do business with and this positive personal relationship eased the way forward to agreements like the INF treaty.

b) i) Key issue: Understanding of historical developments

EXAMINER'S TIP

You are expected to show an understanding of the key developments in relations over the 1950s. Work out whether overall they improved or deteriorated and when the key turning points were. Use the information given to help you. A full answer is expected for 10 marks.

- On the death of Stalin in 1953 many hoped there would be a 'thaw' in the Cold War between East and West, but tensions remained high. When NATO allowed West Germany to join, the USSR responded by forming its own military alliance – the Warsaw Pact.
- However, when Khrushchev established himself as leader, he relaxed Soviet controls over its people and announced a policy of 'peaceful coexistence' with the West. This eased tensions between the USA and USSR.
- This 'thaw' proved brief because of the Soviet crushing of the Hungarian rising in 1956.
- Tensions were further increased when the USA felt they were falling behind the USSR technologically after the Soviet's launched the first Space satellite – Sputnik – in 1957, and put the first man in space – Yuri Gagarin – in 1961.
- However, a real deterioration in relations began in 1960 when the USSR shot down an American U2 spy-plane and captured its pilot. This proved a prelude to two events in 1961 which resulted in a further deterioration in relations.
- In 1961 the USSR hoped to establish control of Berlin. When the USA refused to cooperate, the Berlin Wall was erected. Later that year the USA-sponsored attempt to overthrow Castro in Cuba in the Bay of Pigs invasion failed and Cuba looked to the USSR for help.
- By 1961 USA and USSR relations were as cold as they had been while Stalin was in power. The hopes of a 'thaw' had disappeared.

ii) Key issue: Understanding causation

EXAMINER'S TIP

Focus on giving reasons and supporting them with good evidence. The best answers will set the Cuban Missile Crisis in the wider context of the Cold War.

- The immediate cause of the Cuban Missile Crisis was the siting of Soviet medium-range nuclear missiles in Cuba. These directly threatened most of the USA.
- This Crisis had arisen because after Castro had overturned the US-supported Batista in 1959, the USA had refused to trade with Cuba. Cuba had found a market for its sugar in the USSR and moved closer to the Soviet Union.
- When the American-sponsored attempt to overthrow Castro in the Bay of Pigs fiasco failed, Castro declared himself a Marxist and sought military help from the Soviet Union. That was when the Soviet Union began to build missile sites.
- President Kennedy demanded the destruction of the sites and the removal of the USSR's nuclear missiles and put a naval blockade around Cuba.
- This crisis emerged at a time when US–USSR relations were very poor because of the U2 incident and the building of the Berlin Wall. USA had been humiliated over the U2 incident and could do little to stop the building of the Berlin Wall and was therefore determined not to let Khrushchev get away with missiles in Cuba. Similarly the USA could not back down after the Bay of Pigs fiasco.

CHAPTER 9
The collapse of communism

To revise this topic more thoroughly, see Chapter 9 in *Letts GCSE History Study Guide.*

 Try this sample GCSE question and then compare your answers with the Grade C and Grade A model answers on pages 63 and 64.

This question is about the collapse of Soviet Rule.

a Describe the key features of *Glasnost* and *Perestroika*. [10]

b Why did Gorbachev resign as leader of the USSR in 1991? [15]

You may use the following information to help you with your answer.

- Economic problems
- Problems in Eastern Europe
- Impact of Glasnost and Perestroika
- The role of Boris Yeltsin

Edexcel Specimen Paper, Paper 1, Outline Study A4: 30 minutes

(Total 25 marks)

GRADE C ANSWER

Joanna

(a) Perestroika: Gorbachev realised that Soviet farming and industry were so inefficient that living standards were being left behind by the West ✓ and Russia's huge arms expenditure could not be continued. Perestroika was the economic restructuring of Russia. ✓ It included the encouragement of managers in industry to take the initiative to make their industry prosper, the intention being that they would have to become more efficient, ✓ and the creation of a free market, both for privately produced farm produce and for manufactured goods. ✓

Glasnost: Gorbachev realised that, to compete, Russian society had to encourage freedom of ideas and education, ✓ because otherwise ideas were stifled. This meant freeing political prisoners, ✓ reducing repression by the secret police ✓ and reducing the costs of the state by withdrawing from Afghanistan, ✓ control of Eastern Europe, ✓ the nuclear race and anything else that increased state expenditure (including social provision). ✓

The two definitions are described fluently, in detail. The ideas connect together within each part of the answer.
7/8 marks

(b) With the collapse of Soviet power in Eastern Europe in 1989, Gorbachev was confronted by parts of the USSR itself trying to break away in 1990. ✓ Lithuania, Azerbaijan, Georgia and Russia itself were all calling for independence by the end of that year. ✓ By 1990, the Ukraine was not supplying Leningrad with food, so Leningraders were starving. By 1991 only the Communist Party and the army supported the idea of a USSR, but both thought they had been betrayed by Gorbachev. ✓ They kidnapped him during his summer holiday and tried to retake power by force in Moscow. ✓ Having provoked a huge reaction against themselves, they lost courage and gave up. ✓ Gorbachev was left in charge of a state that had ceased to have any power, and he declared the USSR over, depriving himself of a job. ✓

This is quite a good account of the end of the USSR, but this question demands reasons.
8/15 marks

Grade booster ⋯> move a C to a B
Make sure that you do exactly what is required by the question. The shorter your answer the more precise it needs to be. Joanna may have run out of time on the second part of the question, so she hasn't answered it properly.

The collapse of communism

GRADE A ANSWER

David

(a) In 1985, Russian industry and farming were unprofitable. ✓ Russian society was corrupt, and Russia was bankrupting herself over the arms race and Afghanistan.

While Gorbachev intended to keep Communism, he realised that he needed to restructure Russian agriculture and industry. In his policy of perestroika he allowed Russian farmers to farm for profit ✓ and he encouraged managers in industry to take their own decisions, ✓ encouraging factories to be run profitably and to produce whatever the market wanted. ✓

At the same time, Gorbachev relaxed the controls on the ordinary person. ✓ Political prisoners were released and criticism was encouraged. ✓ This was called 'glasnost'. Abroad this meant new agreements with the USA to reduce nuclear armaments, ✓ and the declaration that the USSR would no longer interfere in Eastern Europe, ✓ all to save money. The withdrawal of Russian forces from Afghanistan was begun. ✓ By 1990 Communism in Eastern Europe had collapsed and in 1990 the two halves of Germany were reunited. ✓

Arguably David could have reduced the first paragraph, which is rather long as an introduction. The other parts are effective in showing the main features of each policy, both inside and outside the USSR.
10/10 marks

(b) Soviet power had never been very popular in Eastern Europe, which had shown this in revolts in Hungary (1956), Czechoslovakia (1968) and Poland (1980). ✓ By 1985 Jaruzelski, in Poland, was gradually losing his authority because of the activities of Solidarity and its successor agitations. ✓ The arrival of Gorbachev and his reforms in the USSR reinforced the position of the agitators in Eastern Europe, and when Gorbachev said that the USSR would no longer impose its own rule, Eastern Europe began to break away, every country opting for free elections during 1989. Gorbachev had lost the Russian Empire. ✓

Within the USSR, Perestroika and Glasnost simply got out of hand. Political as well as economic freedom exposed Gorbachev's mistake — he had thought that the population supported communism, but in fact society broke up under the impact of freedom. ✓ Gorbachev could not keep control at the same time that he reduced military spending. ✓ Lithuania and Azerbaijan demanded independence (which they were guaranteed by the Soviet constitution, should they ask for it). Gorbachev replied with military force in 1990, ✓ but more and more leaders of Soviet republics demanded freedom. Yeltsin was President of Russia, and he wanted freedom, as others did. He said that there was no future in the existence of a Soviet Union. ✓ By 1991, the only support for the continuation of the USSR was among the Communist Party and the military. They tried to regain control by imprisoning Gorbachev at Yalta and taking armed control in August, ✓ but they were opposed by almost the whole population, led by people such as Yeltsin, and they lost their nerve. ✓ The coup was defeated, but Gorbachev never regained his prominence. In December he declared the Soviet Union dead, removing himself from power. ✓

David answers with a considerable amount of detail. The two paragraphs clearly deal with different areas. The second paragraph clearly connects the reasoning with the event in question. The effect is both fluent and fairly stylish.
14/15 marks

>>> **Grade booster** ····> **move A to A***
Fluency and stylishness in your answer are required for top level marks.

QUESTION BANK

① **Détente in the 1970s and 1980s and the collapse of Communism**

Source A
The Solidarity movement sprang forth from the underground scene and toppled the corrupt military regime that was at the time ruling Poland. The eventual success of the Solidarity movement over communism comes as no big surprise since internally the communist party was slowly disintegrating.

(Kristoffer Kalmbach, Poland: The Solidarity Movement and Beyond)

Source B
Hastening to identify itself with Gorbachev, the Jaruzelski team welcomed the spirit of reform wafting from the east and cautiously followed suit at home. By 1988 most political prisoners had been released, unofficial opposition groups were flourishing, and Solidarity, still nominally illegal, operated quite openly.

(from Glenn E. Curtis (ed.), The Library of Congress Country Studies, *Federal Research Division, 1992)*

a) According to **Source A,** why was Solidarity successful in opposing the Communist regime in Poland? ③

b) How did the war in Afghanistan, 1979 to 1989, contribute to the decline of Soviet power? ⑥

c) How reliable to an historian is the view of the decline of Communism in Poland given in **Source B**? ⑥

d) Why did Communism collapse in the Soviet Union, when Gorbachev was leader? Explain your answer. ⑩

AQA B Style, Paper 1: 35 minutes

TOTAL 25

② a) What were the main problems of the Soviet Union when Gorbachev came to power in 1985? ④

b) Why did Gorbachev's reforms cause the collapse of Soviet rule in Eastern Europe? ⑥

c) 'The destruction of the Soviet Union in 1991 was Gorbachev's fault.' How far do you agree with this statement? ⑩

OCR Style, Paper 1: 35 minutes

TOTAL 20

③ **Source A**
We have been fighting in Afghanistan for already six years. If the approach is not changed, we will continue to fight for another 20–30 years … Our military should be told that they are learning badly from this war. What, can it be said that there is no room for our General Staff to manoeuvre? In general, we have not selected the keys to resolving this problem. What, are we going to fight endlessly, as a testimony that our troops are not able to deal with the situation? We need to finish this process as soon as possible.

CPSU CC Politburo transcript, 13 November 1986.

Source B

Yeltsin phoned Yanayev and warned him that 'we don't accept your gang of bandits'. At this point, Yeltsin went outside and climbed atop a tank in front of 20,000 protesters, asking for mass resistance. He denounced the coup as unconstitutional and called for a general strike, declaring himself the 'Guardian of Democracy'. Soon the crowds grew to well over 100,000. Afghan war vets erected barricades in front of the White House and made Molotov cocktails. At the staircase one organizer with a megaphone cried, 'all those courageous who are willing to defend the building, come forward!' The building was surrounded by people from all walks of Russian life, from students and defecting soldiers to priests and pensioners.

(The Failed Coup of 1991)

a) According to **Source A**, why did Russia need to withdraw from Afghanistan? ③

b) How did the war in Afghanistan contribute to Gorbachev's decision to adopt the policies of Glasnost and Perestroika? ⑥

c) How useful to an historian is the view of the Coup of 1991 given in **Source B**? ⑥

d) Why did Communism in Eastern Europe collapse during Gorbachev's time as leader of the USSR?
Explain your answer. ⑩

AQA B Style Question, Paper 1: 35 minutes

TOTAL 25

❶a)   Key issue: Comprehension of Source

EXAMINER'S TIP

Any three relevant points.

- It toppled a 'corrupt military regime'.
- The 'communist party was slowly disintegrating'.
- It was an 'underground' movement, implying popular support.

b)   Key issue: Description of key features and characteristics

EXAMINER'S TIP

Select a few main features and explain each one.

- The war was unsuccessful and a whole generation of conscripts had a part in its failure. It was never popular and most could not understand why the Soviet army was there.
- It showed that as a world superpower, the Soviet Union was actually weak. The quality of her conscripts, and even more importantly, the poor quality of her military planning were shown up.
- It cost too much. The Soviet Union were also having to continue the arms race with the USA and contain Eastern Europe, and military expenditure rose out of control.

c)   Key issue: Evaluation of a Source for reliability

EXAMINER'S TIP

Remember to think who wrote it and why, as well as what it does say, and does not.

- This is an American version of the problem, written soon after the events, so it is likely to have an anti-Soviet bias.
- It does not explain why Soviet policy had changed to leave Jaruzelski free, nor why an old Communist like Jaruzelski should suddenly welcome change.
- It does show a short period of change, which led to the collapse of the Soviet Empire, the next year.

d)   Key issue: Explanation of causation

EXAMINER'S TIP

Stay relevant, use detail, but make a balanced, multicausal answer.

- By the time Gorbachev rose to power, in 1985, the Soviet Union had fallen badly behind the West, both in the productivity of industry and agriculture and in technology. Her population had a lower standard of living, and military expenditure had grown out of control with the nuclear arms race and the war in Afghanistan.
- Gorbachev's policies of Glasnost and Perestroika may well have worked at any other time, but to restructure industry and agriculture at the same time as allowing political freedom and running down the armed forces was foolish.
- The regime was unpopular, because of the failure of the war in Afghanistan and its troubles in Eastern Europe, and Gorbachev made a fundamental mistake in thinking that the people wanted to remain Communist.
- Political freedom allowed states even within the USSR to demand freedom: Lithuania, Georgia, Azerbaijan, even Russia. With the end of dictatorship, Communism itself was disappearing, and with it the reason to keep the Soviet Union together.
- After the failed coup in 1991, the anti-Soviet politicians, such as Yeltsin, had the initiative and the Soviet Union lost all executive importance. Gorbachev dissolved the last vestiges of it, as he resigned in December 1991.

❷a)   Key issue: Recall, select, organise and deploy knowledge

EXAMINER'S TIP

Four short points, or two developed ones.

- Huge arms expenditure: helped to create a low standard of living.
- War in Afghanistan: had destroyed the morale of the USSR.
- Inefficient industry: was old-fashioned and unable to compete with the West.
- Inefficient agriculture: food was poor and expensive but hugely subsidised by the state.

b)   Target: Recall, select, organise and deploy knowledge

EXAMINER'S TIP

Three developed points needed here.

- Gorbachev allowed freedom of political discussion, which undermined the dictatorial

The collapse of communism

style of government, e.g. in Poland, allowing opposition groups, such as Solidarity, to flourish.

- In removing state control of the economy, Gorbachev removed the economic ties that bound Eastern Europe to the Soviet Union.
- In running down military expenditure, Gorbachev removed the threat of Soviet invasion.

c) **Key issue: Recall, select, organise and deploy knowledge.**

EXAMINER'S TIP

A balanced, detailed, fluent answer, showing how causes interrelated.

- In 1985 the Soviet Union was in a seriously weak financial position. She was having to import farm produce from her political enemy, the USA. In addition, arms expenditure and the war in Afghanistan were forcing the government to raise oppressive taxation.
- The Communist system of running the economy from the centre (a command economy) and subsidising her citizens hugely, seemed to have stifled initiative and therefore economic competitiveness. Radical change would be needed to solve these problems.
- Gorbachev took on too many problems at once. He gave political freedom at the same time as trying to restructure economically. The situation got out of hand.
- Gorbachev misunderstood his own people. Given freedom of political expression, they replaced Communism with free institutions. The USSR had no reason for its existence without Communism.
- Given the seriousness of the problems he inherited, Gorbachev failed because he tried to do too much, too quickly.

③a) Key issue: Comprehension of Source

EXAMINER'S TIP

Any three relevant points.

- The war had gone on for six years and 'If the approach is not changed, we will continue to fight for another 20–30 years'.
- The army were not performing well: 'they are learning badly from this war'.
- There were other reasons for withdrawal: 'We need to finish this process as soon as possible.'

b) **Key issue: Description of key features and characteristics**

EXAMINER'S TIP

Select a few main features and explain each one.

- The war was costing huge amounts of money, which could only be raised through high taxes: thus the need for more efficient industry and agriculture.
- The war was destroying the Soviet reputation for military success, creating political uncertainty at home and weakening the Soviet position abroad. Glasnost was thought necessary to disarm critics.
- Russian manufactures, including weaponry, did not work. Restructuring of industry was necessary to create efficiency, both in the war and in exports.

c) **Key issue: Evaluation of a Source for utility.**

EXAMINER'S TIP

Remember to think who wrote it and why, as well as what it does, and does not, say.

- It is not clear what the Sources may be for this account.
- The content seems detailed and includes well-known names, such as Yeltsin, during a well-known incident, so I think it is reliable.
- It only gives details of one incident in Moscow during the failed coup, but does not include information about the plotters or about Gorbachev imprisoned at Yalta.

d) **Key issue: Explanation of causation**

EXAMINER'S TIP

Stay relevant, use detail, but give a balanced, multicausal answer.

- Communism had never been popular in Eastern Europe, as the revolts in Hungary, Czechoslovakia and Poland showed.
- The 1980s were a time of economic hardship throughout the Soviet Empire, probably worse outside the Soviet Union.
- Soviet power was based on military force, but the war in Afghanistan was putting the army under strain. The Soviet Union wanted to withdraw some forces from Eastern Europe.
- Glasnost in the Soviet Union was much the same as more liberal Eastern European governments had always wanted, but not been allowed to have (Dubcek in Prague Spring, 1968).
- Communist governments were unable to enforce a hard-line approach without Soviet troops and at a time when the Soviet Union no longer believed in oppression.
- Gorbachev also declared that he had no intention of intervening.

CHAPTER 10
Britain 1919–1951

To revise this topic more thoroughly, see Chapter 10 in *Letts GCSE History Study Guide.*

 Try this sample GCSE question and then compare your answers with the Grade C and Grade A model answers on pages 70 and 71.

This question is about life in the Depression.

Study the information below and answer the questions which follow.

Information
For many families poverty was so severe during
the 1930s that they had to scavenge for coal

a (i)   Describe the Means Test.   [2]
   (ii) Explain why people went on hunger marches.   [4]
   (iii) How successful were government measures in dealing with the Depression?   [5]
b (i)   Describe the hardship experienced by many women in the depressed areas during the
         1930s.   [3]
   (ii) Explain how people were affected by the growth of car manufacturing during the 1930s.   [4]
c   Were the 1930s a period of depression for all the people of Wales and England? Explain
         your answer fully.   [7]

WJEC A, Specimen Paper, Section B: 30 minutes

(Total 25 marks)

These two answers are at Grade C and A. Compare which one your answer is closest to and think how you could have improved it.

GRADE C ANSWER

This does not explain what the Means Test was, but it shows some recall.
1/2 marks

Who did they intend to protest to?
2/4 marks

Good so far as it goes, but how successful was this?
3/5 marks

A bit more development of how they achieved this would help.
2/3 marks

Yes, but this was not the only way that car manufacturing affected people.
2/4 marks

While she does answer the question, Rebecca has not realised that there were better and worse years during the Depression. Most people could afford to go to the cinema to enjoy the new 'talkie' films and many bought cars. She needs to develop this answer much more.
4/7 marks

Rebecca

(a) (i) The Means Test was hated by the unemployed, because people came into their houses to see what they owned. ✓

(ii) Hunger marchers were protesting about poverty ✓ and unemployment. ✓

(iii) The government helped people to move to areas where there were more jobs, ✓ such as the South of England. ✓

(b) (i) Women had to get used to feeding and clothing their family ✓ on the dole, often themselves going without. ✓

(ii) The pay was better if you could find work in a car factory. ✓

(c) The Depression lasted until war began in 1939. ✓ The worst affected areas were Wales and the North East, ✓ but some were more prosperous, ✓ especially in the South East and Midlands. ✓

Grade booster ···⟩ move a C to a B
Rebecca simply does not make enough points for the number of marks offered. She must develop her answers in more detail to gain top marks.

GRADE A ANSWER

Mark

Two points for two marks.
2/2 marks

(a) (i) From 1931 the Means Test was a way of the government ensuring that the long-term unemployed owned nothing that they could do without, ✓ before giving them assistance. ✓

Keep to reasons.
4/4 marks

(ii) Hunger marches were organised by the trade unions as a method of protest against poverty during the Depression. ✓ Many miners and others were out of work for years and families were unable to survive on the dole. The hunger marches publicised the problem, ✓ attracted charity from onlookers ✓ and allowed people from depressed and more prosperous areas to meet and perhaps to gain understanding of each other. ✓ They brought pressure to bear on the government to do something about the situation. ✓

(iii) The government sponsored public works schemes ✓ and gave basic unemployment pay ✓ but they failed to make much impression on Wales and other depressed areas until rearmament began in 1936. ✓ Then there was a gradual improvement.

Mark has correctly worked out that this question is about Wales, rather than the rest of Britain. An example of a public works scheme would be a useful addition.
4/5 marks

(b) (i) Women often worked if they could find domestic or factory work. ✓ Most were unable to do so, and suffered the worst in the Depression, unable to feed the family ✓ or keep a home together. ✓ They often went hungry themselves, ✓ and had to make do with whatever they could find to clothe their family, depending on charity and jumble sales. ✓

Mark has made too many points here: there are only three marks to give.
3/3 marks

(ii) Many weren't affected at all because they were too poor. ✓ Car manufacturing helped the whole economy and began to stimulate steel, glass and rubber industries as well. ✓ Car workers were well paid ✓ and working conditions were good. ✓ Car owners could commute to work, or take the family out at the week-end, widening horizons. ✓

Again this is an over-full answer, but Mark makes points quickly and effectively.
4/4 marks

(c) As a whole the 1930s was a poor decade, with unemployment peaking at 3 million in 1934 and never going below 1 million before the war. ✓ But it would not be true to say that the whole decade was bad. Generally the economy began to improve before 1939, ✓ largely due to rearmament, and there were always prosperous areas, such as the South East, ✓ where new electrical, car and aeronautical industries flourished. ✓ The spread of the cinema and of car ownership increased the quality of life for many in all areas of the country. ✓ However, in Wales and the North East the declining coal, iron and shipbuilding industries failed to revive. ✓ There was 68% unemployment in Jarrow in 1934 and 62% in Merthyr Tydfil. ✓

This is an excellent answer, showing variation over time and between places, using factual detail well.
7/7 marks

Britain 1919–1951

Grade booster ⋯⟩ move A to A*

Mark could make more use of the question. He is asked whether 'all the people of Wales and England' were in depression. The short answer is that no they were not, because the south-east of England was relatively prosperous. A direct answer given in the terms of the question will score more highly than a generalised one.

1 Study Sources A and B and then answer parts a), b), c) and **either** d) **or** e) which follow.

Source A: The London Blitz in 1940

Source B: The Beveridge Report

The second principle is that organisation of social insurance should be treated as one part only of a comprehensive policy of social progress. Social insurance fully developed may provide income security; it is an attack upon Want. But Want is one only of five giants on the road of reconstruction and in some ways the easiest to attack. The others are Disease, Ignorance, Squalor and Idleness.

(The Beveridge Report: HMSO, 1942)

a) What major problems does **Source A** suggest would have resulted from the war? ③

b) Describe the main reasons why social measures were popular by 1945? ⑤

c) **Using Source B and your own knowledge,** explain the attitude of Sir William Beveridge to the creation of a Welfare State. ⑦

Answer **either** part d) **or** part e).

Either

d) Did the educational reforms created by the National and Labour Governments of 1944–1951 greatly improve the standard of education of the nation? Explain your answer. ⑮

Or

e) Did the industrial and economic policies of the Labour Governments of 1945–1951 have a great impact on life in Britain? ⑮

AQA Style, Paper 2, Section B: 45 minutes

TOTAL 30

2   **This question is about Wales and England after the Second World War.**

Study the information below and answer the questions which follow.

Information

The years after the Second World War saw the introduction of the programme of nationalisation as well as the welfare state.

COAL NATIONALISATION CELEBRATIONS
PROGRAMME OF EVENTS

Empire, Tonypandy Sunday, February 23, 1947	**WORKMEN'S HALL, FERNDALE** *Sunday, February 23rd*
A SACRED CONCERT The Williamson Cleemen The Tonypandy Ladies' Choir	**A SACRED CONCERT** Given by The Pendyrus Male Choir **SUPPORTED BY LOCAL ARTISTS**

a)   i)   Describe what is meant by the term *nationalisation*.   ②

ii)   Explain the purpose of the National Coal Board.   ④

iii)   How successful was Labour's nationalisation policy?   ⑤

b)   i)   Describe the main points of the Beveridge Report.   ③

ii)   Explain the importance of the work of Aneurin Bevan for the people of Wales and England.   ④

c)   Were social and economic conditions better for all the people of Wales and England by 1951?

Explain your answer fully.   ⑦

WJEC A, Section B: 30 minutes

TOTAL 25

①a) **Key issue: Comprehension and inference from a Source**

EXAMINER'S TIP

While the Source may say very little directly, you are expected to infer, or deduce, most of the information.

- The Source shows the destruction of the City of London during the Blitz in 1940. Houses and businesses are on fire, though St Paul's seems unharmed.
- There would have to be a huge rebuilding programme after the war.
- There would have to be compensation for the human tragedies caused by the war.

b) **Key issue: Description of key features and characteristics**

EXAMINER'S TIP

A detailed description of several reasons is expected.

- There was the obvious need to help families harmed by the war.
- There was a determination not to slide back into the poverty of the 1930s. The war had shown that the country could pull together to achieve military victory, now the challenge was full employment.
- The war had mixed people together, who would never have met in ordinary life. The feeling of community was increased. The working classes were felt to have earned the support of the rest of society.

c) **Key issue: Description of key features of a situation and use of a Source**

EXAMINER'S TIP

Concentrate on explaining why Beveridge's attitude was unusual.

- Beveridge was writing early in the war (1942), when victory was still in the balance.
- Beveridge was reporting to the National Government, led by Winston Churchill, an unlikely socialist.
- Beveridge was proposing a 'comprehensive policy of social progress' recommending that the Government should take responsibility for everyone's wellbeing. This radical change would hugely increase Government involvement in everyday life, and looked socialist.

- Beveridge proposed a huge financial responsibility for a government, impoverished and dependent on loans, Americans who would not find this attitude acceptable.

Either

d) **Key issue: Evaluation of extent of change**

EXAMINER'S TIP

You will use several different arguments in your balanced answer, but don't forget to come to a judgement of your own at the end.

- The Butler Education Act raised the school leaving age to 15 and created a system of secondary education open to all without fees.
- It introduced an exam, the 11+, which decided whether the pupil would move on to a grammar, technical or secondary modern school.
- O Levels and A Levels replaced the old School Certificate system.
- An 'examination ladder' would allow the best to continue on towards university.
- A huge school-building and teacher education programme had to be created to achieve this.
- But the 'examination ladder' implied that most children would fail at some stage and be relegated to less acceptable schools (the secondary moderns) or to industry. Only academic ability seemed to matter.
- The 11+ exam was a particularly poor method of making a final decision on people's futures.

Or

e) **Key issue: Evaluation of extent of change**

EXAMINER'S TIP

Use several different arguments in your balanced answer, but don't forget the judgement at the end.

- The nationalisation of coal, public transport, iron and steel, etc. was intended to permit more effective planning and cooperation between industries and to ensure fair treatment of their employees.
- In the short term nationalisation was both popular and effective in curing the problems

of those industries after the war. Probably private investment would have been insufficient to have revived them on its own.

- In the longer term, governments would run these industries uncompetitively and fail to take the hard decisions necessary to keep them profitable.
- Labour's financial policies also had mixed results. In 1946 they nationalised the Bank of England. The USA had already withdrawn her loans, yet British industry needed investment to return it to peacetime production and had lost her markets abroad during the war.
- The Labour Government send J. M. Keynes to negotiate a new loan with the USA, which he was only partly able to achieve. Though industry quickly recovered and increased exports, imports remained very high. The country was going bankrupt.
- Only the receipt of Marshall Aid in 1947 and 1948 allowed recovery to be completed.
- When the Labour Government fell in 1951, food rationing was still more severe than it had been during the Battle of Britain.

2 a) i) **Key issue: Recall and description of events/issues**

EXAMINER'S TIP

For 2 marks, keep this to a short definition.

- Labour party policy to take public ownership of major industries.

ii) **Key issue: Explanation of key events and issues.**

EXAMINER'S TIP

Develop this by saying what was wrong before.

- National Coal Board established because of the unpopularity of the coalowners, the need to rationalise the industry, the demands of the trade unions, to improve conditions, etc.

iii) **Key issue: Analysis and explanation of key events and issues**

EXAMINER'S TIP

Keep this judgement to the short term, within the date range of the topic.

- Labour nationalised most of heavy industry and public transport.
- They were able to reorganise industry after the ravages of war and the depression, making large-scale investments which private owners could not have afforded.

- Though the move was successful in the short term, it was opposed by the Conservative Party, business and the press.

b)i) **Key issue: Recall and description of key events and issues**

EXAMINER'S TIP

Some detail is necessary here, not just a bald statement.

- The Beveridge Report identified the Five Giants of Want, Disease, Ignorance, Squalor and Idleness.
- It led to the creation of the Welfare State by the postwar Labour government.
- The Welfare State included the NHS, Family Allowances, National Insurance and improved educational provision.

ii) **Key issue: Explanation of key events and issues**

EXAMINER'S TIP

You don't need a complete biography here, just the main points.

- He was Labour Minister of Health and founded the National Health Service.
- He went on to be Minister of Housing and was responsible for the huge house-building programme.
- Both of these achievements greatly improved the lives of ordinary people.

c) **Key issue: Explanation, analysis and evaluation of key events and issues**

EXAMINER'S TIP

You need a balanced and fairly detailed answer.

- Housing, health care and wage levels were better for most people than they had been in 1945.
- The effects of the 1944 Butler Education Act were also being felt.
- Industry had largely been reorganised after the war and export markets regained.
- Rationing remained, government control of industry was excessive, taxation of the better off was very high and many doubted whether Britain would continue to prosper without more freedom.

Russia
1914–1941

To revise this topic more thoroughly, see Chapter 11 in *Letts GCSE History Study Guide.*

 Try this sample GCSE question and then compare your answers with the Grade C and Grade A model answers on pages 77 and 78.

Study the Sources carefully, and then answer the questions which follow.

Source A

They receive miserable wages, and generally live in an overcrowded state, very commonly in special lodging houses. A woman takes several rooms in her own name, subletting each one; and it's common to see ten or even more persons living in one room and four sleeping on one bed. The normal working day … is eleven and a half hours of work, exclusive of meal times. But … manufacturers receive permission to work overtime, so that the average day is longer … fourteen or fifteen hours.

(from G. Gapon, The Story of my Life, *Chapman and Hall, 1905)*

Source B

24 July 1916

The most important and immediate question is fuel and metal – iron and copper for ammunition. Without metals the mills cannot supply a sufficient amount of bullets and bombs. The same is true in regard to the railways. Trepov [Minister of Transportation] assures me that the railways work better this year than last and produces proof, but nevertheless every one complains that they are not doing as well as they might.

(Tsar Nicholas II)

Source C

The march to commemorate International Women's Day on 23 February 1917

Use the Sources and your own knowledge to explain your answers to these questions.

a   Study **Source A**. Explain why opposition was growing in Russia before 1914.   [7]

b   Study **Source B**. How far does this Source explain how the First World War weakened Tsarism?   [7]

c   Study **Source C**. Does this photograph support or oppose the interpretation that the Russian Revolution began as a bread riot?   [6]

OCR B Style, Paper 1, Section B (first question): 35 minutes

(Total 20 marks)

These two answers are at Grade C and A. Compare which one your answer is closest to and think how you could have improved it.

GRADE C ANSWER

Christopher

(a) Source A shows how bad conditions were for workers in Russia before 1914. It mentions the miserable wages, the overcrowded lodging houses and fourteen or fifteen hour days. It also shows the reason for anger at the factory bosses who expect so much or at the landladies who pack so many people into their rooms.

Christopher does well to get so much information out of the Source, but this is not enough because he makes no additional points of his own.
4/7 marks

(b) The Russian Army was being defeated because they were not supplied with enough rifles and bullets. This source shows Tsar Nicholas complaining about the shortage of bullets and bombs and he even says that the railways are in trouble. No wonder that the soldiers were ready to revolt.

Christopher's lack of extra knowledge is a real problem. What other reasons were there for the weakening of Tsarism during the War?
3/7 marks

(c) The Source seems to show the front of a long procession of women, led by a banner, which I cannot read. The caption says that it was commemorating International Women's Day, which I know was the first demonstration in the Revolution. It does not seem to show a bread riot, but it does not show much to do with revolution either.

Christopher has analysed this quite well, using the photograph, the caption and his own knowledge to connect the picture with the Revolution. However, he could not remember the importance of the bread riot to these events.
5/6 marks

> ### Grade booster ⋯⟩ move a C to a B
> It is not enough to analyse the Source. To get higher marks you must revise well so that you can give details of the other side of the argument from your own knowledge.

Russia 1914–1941

Premila

A good answer which both uses the Source and her own knowledge. She kept clearly to the theme of reasons for the revolution and gave several from her own knowledge.
7/7 marks

(a) Opposition was growing in Russia for many reasons, but Source A shows only some of them. It mentions low wages, ✓ overcrowding and the length of the working day ✓ as being important reasons for industrial discontent, but it doesn't mention the loss of the 1905 Russo-Japanese War, ✓ the way the Tsar ignored and reduced the influence of the Duma, ✓ the incompetence and corruption of the administration, ✓ or the repressive and cruel conduct of the regime. It shows how the actions of a small-scale capitalist would cause resentment, ✓ but does not show any of the agricultural grievances.

While this is a good answer, Premila probably makes a tactical mistake in connecting all her reasons for the weakening of Tsarism with this one Source. She would have scored better if she had mentioned some that were unconnected, such as the dislike of Tsarina Alexandra's government at home and the influence of Rasputin.
5/7 marks

(b) Source B dates from the time that the Tsar was at the Army HQ, trying to solve the problem of supply that had been so serious in 1915. ✓ It shows the shortage of basic necessities was still continuing – that the shortage of iron and copper was holding back production of bullets and bombs ✓ and that there was a continuing problem of transportation by railway. ✓ It also shows that 'everyone' was complaining and that Nicholas thought it was his responsibility to solve the problem. ✓ In its context, this source is useful in explaining that, by 1916, the real war was being fought in terms of factory production and transport at home, without which the troops could not fight. ✓ The revolution would begin because the Tsar was blamed for every inefficiency, because of the intolerable strain put on the industrial workforce, because of the lack of food resulting from the breakdown of the train network and because of the breakdown of the economy in supplying everything. Much of this is not fully explained in this source. ✓

This uses the Source intelligently, explaining both what it can and what it cannot prove. Premila's own knowledge is sufficient to connect it with the Revolution. Premila cannot read the writing on the banner but, as with any source which is unreadable, she will not lose through that. She has made a sensible decision as to what it must say from other evidence.
5/6 marks

(c) The Source seems to show quite an orderly demonstration, rather than a riot. ✓ I cannot tell what the banner is saying, but the caption explains that this happened on International Women's Day, ✓ so the demonstration, which is mostly by women, seems to be connected with this, rather than with bread, or with revolution, for that matter. ✓ However, I know from my own knowledge that this demonstration was the beginning of the Revolution, ✓ that it got out of hand and turned into a bread riot. So, while this does not directly prove that the Revolution began as a bread riot, it does not disprove it either. ✓

Grade booster ⋯⋯> move A to A*
Always comment both on what the Source does say and on what it does not. To explain its limitations you must have plenty of your own knowledge to measure it against.

QUESTION BANK

1 Study **Sources A to E** and then answer **all** parts of the question which follow.

Source A: A demonstration in July 1917

Troops loyal to the Provisional Government fire on demonstrators in July 1917

Source B: The Provisional Government is abandoned

The hours of the night dragged on painfully. From everywhere we expected reinforcements, but none appeared. There were endless telephone negotiations with the Cossack regiments. Under various excuses the Cossacks stubbornly stuck to their barracks, asserting all the time that 'everything would be cleared up' within fifteen or twenty minutes and that they would then 'begin to saddle their horses'... Meanwhile the night hours passed.

(from A. Kerensky, The Catastrophe, *Appleton and Co. (NY), 1927)*

Source C: Bolshevik support among the Garrison

An order was sent out through the garrison from Smolny ... Officers not recognising the authority of the Military Revolutionary Committee to be arrested. The commanders of many regiments fled of their own accord. In other units the officers were removed and arrested.

(from L. Trotsky, History of the Russian Revolution, *Vol. III, Gollancz, 1932–33)*

Source D: An interpretation of the Storming of the Winter Palace

(A 1937 painting by a Soviet artist, Sokolov-Skayla)

Source E: An American interpretation of the Assault on the Winter Palace
The Women's Death Battalion stayed on. By midnight, the defense was reduced to them and a handful of teenage cadets guarding the Malachite Room. When no more gunfire issued from the palace, the Red Guards and sailors cautiously drew near. The first to penetrate were sailors and troops of the Pavlovskii Regiment who clambered through open windows on the Hermitage side. Others made their way through unlocked gates. The Winter Palace was not taken by assault ... In reality, the Winter Palace was overrun by mobs after it had ceased to defend itself. The total casualties were five killed and several wounded, most of them victims of stray bullets.

(from Richard Pipes, The Russian Revolution 1899–1919, *Fontana, 1992)*

a) Explain what you can learn from **Source A** about the popularity of the Provisional Government in July 1917. ⑤

b) Compare **Source B** and **Source C**. Are they agreeing about why the Provisional Government failed to gain help from the army? ⑥

c) How reliable is **Source B** as evidence about the fall of the Provisional Government? Explain your answer using **Source B and your own knowledge**. ⑨

d) **Sources D and E** give different interpretations of the assault on the Winter Palace in 1917.

  Why do you think these interpretations are so different?
  Explain your answer using **Sources D and E and your own knowledge**. ⑩

e) **Use your own knowledge** to explain how successful Lenin was in imposing Bolshevik control on Russia in the years 1918–1924. ⑮

AEB Specification B style, Paper 2, Section A: 1 hour

TOTAL 45

❷ **The rise and fall of the the Communist state: the Soviet Union, 1928–91**
This question is about Stalin's rule in the Soviet Union in the period 1928 to 1945. Look at the photograph below of an industrial city and then answer all the questions which follow.

Magnitogorsk in production

a) Give ONE reason to explain why Russian industry was far behind the West in 1928. ③

b) Describe the key features of the First Five Year Plan. ⑤

c) Why did Stalin increase political persecution in the years from 1928–1939? ⑤

d) What were the effects of Stalin's economic policies in the years to 1941? ⑦

Edexcel Specification A style, Paper 1: 1 hour

TOTAL 20

①a) **Key issue: Comprehension and inference from a Source**

EXAMINER'S TIP

Just use Source A. Don't make any points just from your own knowledge.

- This demonstration took place only four months after the Provisional Government took power, so something was already very wrong. The news of the Kerensky Offensive had destroyed confidence in the Government.
- The picture shows troops firing on the demonstrators against the liberal principles of the Provisional Government which shocked the population. You can see that the demonstration had not protected itself against machine guns.
- The crowd does not appear to be threatening the soldiers, firing from the left. Was this violence unjustified?

b) **Key issue: Comparison of Sources to detect similarities and differences**

EXAMINER'S TIP

While it is easy to see the differences, do they necessarily disagree?

- While Source B mentions Cossack Regiments, Source C does not. While Source C mentions the arrest of officers, Source B does not, etc.
- The Sources agree that the Provisional Government had lost control of the military forces and therefore that no help was likely to come from them. Source C probably explains the lack of cooperation in Source B.

c) **Key issue: Evaluation of the Source for reliability in context**

EXAMINER'S TIP

Who wrote it? When and why? How does it compare with other sources or your own knowledge?

- Kerensky was the Prime Minister of the Provisional Government. He wrote this in 1927, 10 years after the event, and would probably try to cover up his own responsibility for losing power.

- This Source suggests that the reinforcements were expected, that it was their duty to arrive. It could be interpreted as being their fault that the Provisional Government fell, or it could be that Kerensky was deluded in expecting their support.
- Source C suggests developments of which Kerensky was ignorant.

d) **Key issue: Analysis and evaluation of interpretations**

EXAMINER'S TIP

First look at the Sources to identify the interpretations from the evidence, then explain why, using your own knowledge as well as the Sources themselves.

- Source D is a Soviet interpretation of 1937, showing the mythical heroic storming of the Winter Palace as the achievement of the masses.
- Source E is a modern American interpretation, eager to suggest that the 'storming' of the Winter Palace was gradual, relatively peaceful and without opposition, destroying the Soviet myth.

e) **Key issue: Evaluation of extent of change**

EXAMINER'S TIP

Don't just describe what Lenin did as a narrative. Try to make a 'before and after' comparison.

- Lenin had ended Russian involvement in the First World War, at great cost to Russia, but had won back most of her losses during the Russian Civil War.
- Lenin had given the land to the peasants.
- Lenin had imposed Communism, at first in the extreme form of 'War Communism' but by 1924 he was having more success with the moderate form in NEP.
- Lenin had constructed a Communist dictatorship, complete with prison camps and a secret police force that could shoot suspects without trial.
- Lenin had failed to create the ideal state which Communism promised.
- The Soviet Union was surrounded by enemy capitalist states and world revolution had failed.

a) **Key issue: Explanation of causation/recall of knowledge**

EXAMINER'S TIP

Develop one point with additional knowledge.

- Since the First World War, Russian industry had been isolated from Western trade.
- This was because most countries refused to deal with a Communist country, which did not honour its debts.

b) **Key issue: Key features/recall of knowledge**

EXAMINER'S TIP

Don't just list here, give an overall interpretation too.

- Targets were to be set centrally, to be achieved within five years.
- Heavy industry: coal, iron, steel, machinery were expanded at the expense of consumer industries such as shoes and clothes.
- Huge new factories were created, such as Stalingrad tractors.
- Much effort was put into communications (Belomore Canal) and electrification (Magnitogorsk).
- Much was achieved, and the Plan was declared complete in four years, but wilder targets were not met. The foundations for further advance had been laid, but the standard of living was not improved.

c) **Key issue: Analysis of causation and motivation**

EXAMINER'S TIP

Show that you are aware of everything else that is happening, e.g. the threat of Trotskyism, rise of Hitler, collectivisation, etc.

- From the beginning of this period, Stalin was scared of internal dissent, especially opposition from 'Trotskyists'. Trotsky had been exiled abroad and was being very energetic in criticising Stalin's policies. Stalin thought that he still had huge support inside the USSR.
- Stalin feared 'capitalist' countries and thought that the USSR must defend herself with large armed forces and constant vigilance against spies and 'saboteurs' at home. Hitler's Germany was an obvious threat during these years.

- Industrialisation and collectivisation were imposed by force from the centre and against huge opposition, especially from the richer peasants or 'kulaks'. Stalin was afraid of the consequences.
- Even within the Communist Party, many thought Stalin's policies were too severe, e.g. Kamenev, Bukharin. In 1934 there was a move to replace Stalin with Kirov: Kirov was murdered. Most of the old leadership, Stalin's rivals, were murdered after show trials from 1936, along with thousands of others from important positions.

d) **Key issue: Consequences/recall of knowledge**

EXAMINER'S TIP

Don't just look at short-term economic effects. What were the longer term results of these policies?

- Very gradual increases in production through collectivisation (about 20% higher than 1928) was arguably less than if Stalin had left agriculture alone.
- The collectivised peasantry was not loyal when Russia was invaded in 1941.
- The Communist government had taken political control of the countryside.
- Industrial production had increased 700% on 1928, but heavy industry had outstripped light so that the standard of living had not risen as steeply as this suggests.
- Heavy industry, by 1940, was 15 times more productive than in 1913 and had changed the balance of power between Germany and the USSR. Though Germany began by winning in her invasion of Russia, she was fought off and invaded in her turn. The USSR had become a superpower.

FOR MORE INFORMATION ON THIS TOPIC ... SEE REVISE GCSE HISTORY ... CHAPTER 11

CHAPTER 12

Germany 1918–1945

To revise this topic more thoroughly, see Chapter 12 in *Letts GCSE History Study Guide.*

 Try this sample GCSE question and then compare your answers with the Grade C and Grade A model answers on pages 84–86.

Study Sources A and B and then answer parts **a**, **b**, **c** and either **d** or **e**

Source A: Part of a report written in 1922 by an American diplomat about Hitler

Adolf Hitler has from the first been the dominating force in the Nazi movement, and the personality of this man has undoubtedly been one of the most important factors contributing to its success. His ability to influence an assembly is uncanny. In private conversation he is a forceful and logical speaker, which when coupled with a fanatical earnestness, made a very deep impression.

Source B: Part of the Nazi Party's twenty-five point programme 1920

1   We demand the union of all Germans to form a greater Germany.
2   We demand the abolition of the Peace Treaty of Versailles.
3   We demand land and territory for the nourishment of our people.
4   None but those of German blood may be members of the German nation. No Jew, therefore, may be a member of the nation.
5   We demand the creation of a strong central government in Germany.

a   What can you learn from **Source A** about Adolf Hitler's leadership of the party?   [3]
b   **Using Source B and your own knowledge**, explain which sorts of people were attracted
         to the Nazi Party in the 1920s.   [7]
c   Describe how Hitler tried to seize power in the Munich Putsch of 1923.   [5]

Answer **either** part **d** or part **e**

Either

d   Did the Nazi Party have so little success in the 1920s because the Weimar government
         was successful? Explain your answer.   [15]

Or

e   Why did the Nazi Party win so much support between 1929 and 1933?   [15]

AQA Style Question, Paper 2, Section B: 45 minutes

(Total 30 marks)

GRADE C ANSWER

Germany 1918–1945

This does try to answer the question and gives lots of reasons for the success of the Nazi Party between 1929 and 1933. There is a little supporting evidence for one or two of the reasons given. However, there are two weaknesses. First, Shaiza does not develop her reasons by giving good supporting evidence. Secondly, she does not suggest whether some reasons are more important than others.

8/15 marks

Shaiza (answer to option **(e)** only shown here)

(e) There are lots of reasons why support for the Nazi Party increased between 1929 and 1933. ✓ Hitler was a great speaker and Nazi propaganda was excellent. ✓ Hitler could rally support and enthusiasm with his speeches and once flew all over Germany making speeches. ✓ Nazi posters and rallies won support also. ✓ Torchlight processions and uniforms attracted many as did promises of work and to overturn the Treaty of Versailles. ✓

The Great Depression helped as well as did the weakness of the Weimar government. ✓ People also feared a communist revolution. ✓

Grade booster ····> move a C to a B

To improve, Shaiza must explain her reasons more carefully by giving some supporting detailed evidence. For example, supporting her point about the Great Depression by giving some information about its impact on Germany (6 million unemployed) and showing how the Weimar Government and moderate parties failed to come up with any solutions.

Philip

(a) The source indicates that Hitler was the leading figure in the Nazi movement and that one reason for this was his personality which could win over people by a combination of emotional force, logic and fanaticism. ✓ The source also suggests that his leadership in the Nazi movement was also to do with his ability to sway a crowd with his speaking. ✓

Philip has shown a good understanding of the Source and has drawn out two key elements.
3/3 marks

(b) This extract from the 25 points highlights the nationalist ✓ ideas associated with the extreme right. Whilst the second point about abolishing the Treaty of Versailles would have met with general approval, ✓ many may have been put off by the other ideas here which suggested that Germany might expand. Democrats, too, would have been concerned about the idea of strong government, ✓ which might mean dictatorship. The kind of people who would have been attracted by the points here were extreme right-wing nationalists who believed the 'stab in the back' explanation for Germany's defeat in the war and who had some sympathy for the anti-Semitic views implied in point 4.

Philip has not only understood and used the Source material, but has also set this in the context of his own knowledge of the period. A number of aspects are explained. To get to the highest mark the candidate might have mentioned something about the points not included here. For example he could have added a sentence like the following: 'However, this extract does not include the more 'socialist' aspects of the 25 points which were designed to attract German workers'.
6/7 marks

(c) Hitler hoped to take over the Bavarian government and then march on Berlin and overthrow the Weimar government. ✓ The attempt was made in November 1923 after the government had called off the popular passive resistance taking place in protest at the French invasion of the Ruhr. ✓ However, the coup was a disastrous failure because Hitler failed to win the support of the army and the police. Having marched into a Munich beer hall and apparently persuaded local leaders to support him, Hitler, the next day, marched with his followers into Munich where they were stopped by the local police. ✓ Some Nazis were shot in the confrontation, but Hitler escaped only to be arrested later and then be put on trial. ✓

Philip has shown a good understanding of the Munich putsch and has described a number of different aspects of the attempted coup. This has started well. Philip has shown good knowledge and understanding of the period and has explained the impact of Weimar success in the later 1920s. Note how he has supported his ideas with examples.
5/5 marks

(d) The Nazi Party were an extreme right-wing nationalist party opposed to the fragile democratic system set up in Germany in the wake of defeat in the First World War. Like other extreme parties such as the left-wing Communist Party they could only hope to win a lot of support at times of crisis. ✓ However, after the Weimar Republic had survived the intense problems following the war (hyperinflation, invasion and attempted coups by left and right, including the Munich Putsch), it appeared to achieve economic and political stability during the second half of the 1920s. ✓ This was largely due to the economic measures taken in the aftermath of the Ruhr invasion with the Dawes Plan providing the stimulus for

Philip has chosen the first option on this question.

foreign investment and the Rentenmark bringing an end to hyperinflation. It also seemed that Gustav Stresemann was achieving success in foreign affairs by securing reconciliation with France at Locarno and German entry to the League of Nations. The period of violent politics and constant elections seemed to be over. The Nazis only gained 14 seats in the 1924 election and just 12 in 1928. ✓

However, the recovery of the Weimar Republic was not the only reason why the Nazi Party enjoyed so little success in the 1920s. ✓ It was also because it was one of a number of small extremist parties and had no national support for much of the period. Even in its base - Bavaria - its support was limited. For example, when Hitler joined the party it had less than 20 members and in 1923 Hitler failed to mobilise mass support for his attempted coup. ✓ The failure of the Munich Putsch can also be seen as a reason for limited success because the Nazi Party had shown itself to be incompetent and extremist and other right-wing politicians distanced themselves from it. ✓ What is more, as political stability returned after 1923 there was little support for a party associated with street violence and attempts to overthrow democracy. ✓ The second half of the 1920s was spent by Hitler in reorganising the party so that it would later be in a position to win nationwide support and try to win power not by force but through elections. That organisation was there in 1928 but the political and economic conditions were not right - the Weimar government was relatively stable and economic prosperity was still increasing. ✓

This is an effective paragraph because Philip has gone beyond the reason given in the question to provide further reasons and support them with evidence. Because he has provided a multicausal and supported answer it would score highly.
12/15 marks

Grade booster ····⟩ move A to A*

Philip could write a final paragraph which reaches a reasoned conclusion on the balance between the various reasons. For example: 'For an extreme right wing anti-democratic party like the Nazis to succeed required political instability and economic crisis in order to undermine the existing system. Although these conditions were there between 1919 and 1923 the Nazi Party was too small and localised to achieve success. However, as it organised on a national basis the Weimar Republic experienced a period of prosperity and stability which left the Nazis without the potential for mass support.'

1 **Establishing the Nazi dictatorship and controlling the German people**

Study Sources A to D and then answer all parts of the question which follow.

Source A: The results of the Reichstag election on 5 March 1933

Party	Seats
Nazis	288
Nationalists	52
Centre	74
Social Democrats	120
Communists	81

Source B: Hitler explains his reasons for the Night of the Long Knives, July 1934
It became clear that my SA were planning a revolution to seize power. I alone was able to solve the problem. In order to save the state the SA had to be destroyed.

Source C: A historian comments on the reasons for the Night of the Long Knives, July 1934
If Hitler was to secure their support for his succession to the Presidency, the Army in return were determined to get the removal of the SA threat to take over the Army.

Source D: A British cartoon commenting on the Night of the Long Knives, July 1934

'They salute with both hands now!'

Source E: A British newspaper comments on the consequences of the Night of the Long Knives, 2 July 1934
It is not likely that the swift collapse of the Nazi government will be prevented as a result of the spectacular crushing this weekend of the mysterious revolt of the SA leaders. Nazism is discredited among large sections of the German people.

a) Explain what you can learn about the Reichstag elections of 5 March 1933 from Source A. ⑤

b) Compare the reasons for the Night of the Long Knives according to Sources B and C. ⑥

c) How useful is Source D for studying the Night of the Long Knives? ⑨

d) How accurate an interpretation is Source E of the effects of the Night of the Long Knives? Explain your answer **using Source E and your own knowledge**. ⑩

e) **Use your own knowledge** to explain how successful Hitler was in controlling the German people in the period 1934–1939. ⑮

AQA Style Paper 2, Section A: 60 minutes

TOTAL 45

2 a) Describe Nazi policies towards women. ④

b) Explain why Hitler paid so much attention to young people. ⑥

c) 'The main reason why there was little opposition to the Nazis was fear of the SS and Gestapo.' Do you agree with this statement? Explain your answer. ⑩

OCR Style Question, Paper 1: 35 minutes

TOTAL 20

3 This question is about how Hitler dealt with opposition. Look carefully at Sources A–E and then answer questions a) to d) below.

Source A: Statistics about the victims of the Nazi police state

Death sentences for 'political oppression':	1930–32	8
	1934–39	534
Number under 'protective arrest' in 1939:		162 734
Number in concentration camps in 1939:		21 400

Source B: The aims of the Gestapo according to the deputy chief of the Gestapo
Any attempt to gain recognition for, or even uphold, different ideas [to the Nazis] will be ruthlessly dealt with as the symptom of an illness which threatens the healthy unity of the state.

To discover the enemies of the state, watch them and render them harmless at the right moment is the duty of a political police.

In order to fulfil this duty, the political police must be free to use every means suited to achieve the desired end.

Source C: From a school textbook about Nazi Germany
The Gestapo had been set up in 1933 by Goering. Its purpose was to discover the enemies of the Nazi state using whatever means they thought necessary; in other words they could break the law. Arrests late at night, interrogation, torture, imprisonment and sometimes death: these were the hallmarks of the Gestapo operations. They instilled fear in those thinking of resistance.

Source D: A British cartoon about the Night of the Long Knives, July 1934

Source E: A photograph showing Nazi stormtroopers arresting suspected Communists in 1933

a) Study Source A. What can you learn from Source A about how the Nazis dealt with opposition? ④

b) Study Sources A, B and C. Do Sources A and B support the evidence of Source C? Explain your answer. ⑥

c) Study Sources D and E. How useful are these two Sources as evidence about how Hitler dealt with opposition? ⑧

d) Study all the Sources. 'Hitler's policies were totally effective in eliminating all opposition.' Use these Sources, and your own knowledge, to explain whether you agree with this view. ⑫

TOTAL 30

QUESTION BANK ANSWERS

1 a) **Key issue: Comprehension and inference from a Source**

EXAMINER'S TIP

This question only requires a fairly brief answer of four or five sentences. Say what the Source shows and draw one or two inferences from it by using your own knowledge.

- This table shows that the Nazi Party won 288 seats in the Reichstag elections. This was many more seats than any other party. So the Nazis won the election.
- Although the Nazi Party were the largest party they still did not have a majority in the Reichstag (other parties had 327 seats), so they would not be able to pass laws without the support of another party such as the right-wing Nationalists.

b) **Key issue: Comparison of Sources**

EXAMINER'S TIP

The aim here is to identify similarities and differences. Again a long answer is not required – four or five sentences would be fine.

- Source B says that Hitler got rid of the SA because they were planning a revolution whereas Source C claims Hitler had to get rid of the SA in order to win the support of the army for him becoming president.
- Both sources see the SA as a threat either to the army or directly to Hitler, but Source C indicates there were other motives (such as winning the support of the army) besides getting rid of the SA threat.

c) **Key issue: Evaluation of Source for utility**

EXAMINER'S TIP

Don't merely comment on what information the Source contains, but also assess how useful the Source is in terms of its provenance, reliability or bias. It is important that you recognise both the strengths and limitations of the Source. Take care to ensure you not only make points but support them by reference to the Source and the information given about it.

- It is accurate in so far as it shows the submission of the SA and the guns of the SS and the body of Ernst Röhm, leader of the SA.
- This is a political cartoon seeking to make a point about Hitler's regime; it is not meant to be an accurate portrayal of events and in this respect is therefore of limited use.
- However, it does give a British view (in a British newspaper) of what has happened and of Hitler – he is a thug (hence 'smoking gun') who has asserted his authority by force.

d) **Key issue: Analysis and evaluation of interpretation**

EXAMINER'S TIP

Do not just summarise the Source content. To score well you will need to assess the Source in relation to its authorship, date, audience and possible bias. You will also need to assess it against what you know of the consequences of the Night of the Long Knives.

- This is an interpretation in the immediate aftermath of the event, before the consequences could really be known and, perhaps, before all the facts were known.
- It is also in a British newspaper and by a journalist who may not possess all the relevant information (there is a reference to 'mysterious events'). His assertion about the impact of the event on the German people ('Nazism is discredited') is not supported by any evidence and did not appear to be borne out by subsequent events.
- Certainly the journalist was wrong because the Nazi regime did not collapse. Indeed Hitler went on to consolidate his power by making himself Führer and winning the loyalty of the army.

e) **Key issue: Evaluation of the extent of success using own knowledge**

EXAMINER'S TIP

This question does not require you to use the Sources and its focus is on the period after 1934. You are expected to write three or four paragraphs where points are supported with examples. Adopt a 'for and against' approach so that you can come to a balanced conclusion about the degree of success Hitler had.

- The Nazis used a number of methods to control the German people: propaganda, censorship, spies and informers, the Gestapo and SS, a Nazified court system and concentration camps.
- Propaganda flooded the German people with the Nazi message, whilst censorship of all

media from newspapers to sculpture denied opposition the oxygen of publicity.

- Spies, informers and the activities of the Gestapo – with people disappearing and dawn raids – helped create a climate of fear which silenced potential opposition. People were afraid to speak out for fear of the concentration camp.
- The Nazis also attempted to control both people's working lives and their leisure time through the DAF and other organisations.
- As a result there was little open opposition and few serious attempts to oppose Hitler. However, the success was not total. The numbers under arrest and in concentration camps suggest there was opposition and there is much evidence of quiet resistance by, for example, 'forgetting' to say 'Heil Hitler!' There was even some resistance among young people in the 'Swing' movement.

2 a) Key issue: To demonstrate knowledge and understanding

EXAMINER'S TIP

There are two ways to get to full marks: either make four separate points about Nazi policies towards women, or make two main points and support them with accurate detail.

- Nazis encouraged women to give up work because they believed their purpose was to bear and bring up good Aryan children and look after the home.
- The Nazis encouraged women to have children by offering incentives such as loans which did not have to be repaid if a woman had four children. They also offered medals.
- The Nazis discouraged make-up and instead idealised the traditional plain country girl image.
- Girls were brought up and educated to be the mothers of future Aryan children.

b) Key issue: Explanation of reasons

EXAMINER'S TIP

You will need to identify two or three reasons and explain them with some supporting evidence or development.

- Hitler saw the young as particularly open to his ideas. Older people were difficult to change, but the young could be moulded. That is why Hitler was concerned both to control what went on in school and, through the Hitler Youth, what happened in young people's leisure time.

- Hitler also saw the youth as the future Aryan super-race who would fight for and build the German Empire which he hoped would last a thousand years. He needed therefore to indoctrinate the young with his racial ideas and to encourage a warlike spirit and habit of obedience.

c) Key issue: Evaluation of an issue

EXAMINER'S TIP

You will need to construct an essay so some thinking time is important.
You must deal with the 'main reason' and explain its importance. However, you must balance this against other reasons. To get the top marks you must come to a balanced conclusion which links reasons together and explains why you think one main reason on its own could not provide a satisfactory explanation.

- Fear of the Gestapo and the SS was certainly important in limiting opposition. The Gestapo had wide powers of arrest and kept a network of spies and informers. People would be arrested in dawn raids or simply disappeared. Many ended up in concentration camps policed by the SS.
- Propaganda and censorship also prevented opposition. Propaganda was everywhere, on the radio, in the newspapers, in posters and even through the films seen at the cinema. Censorship, which extended to everything from sculpture to jokes, starved potential opposition of publicity.
- Under the Enabling Law Hitler was able to pass decrees banning trade unions, and all other political parties. He also Nazified the courts by appointing Nazi judges. Opposition was therefore difficult to organise and could be punished severely.
- But many people did not want to oppose the Nazis because they viewed Hitler as a saviour who brought work, bread and pride back to Germany. Unemployment disappeared and Hitler succeeded in reversing the Treaty of Versailles.
- There is no one reason why the Nazis faced so little opposition. Certainly the climate of fear created by the activities of the Gestapo and the SS would have stifled much potential opposition, but one reason it was successful was the combination of propaganda and censorship which denied opposition the oxygen of publicity. The apparent success of the Nazis too in solving Germany's problems probably persuaded many to accept the darker side of Nazi rule and keep their criticisms to themselves.

a) Key issue: Comprehension of a Source

EXAMINER'S TIP

This requires only a short answer of three or four sentences. You should make statements based on the information in the Source and then suggest what you might conclude from the information.

- The Source tells us that some opponents were put to death, some were taken into 'protective custody' and some were put into concentration camps.
- The large numbers of people involved here might indicate that opposition was dealt with severely by the Nazis.

b) Key issue: Corroboration by cross-referencing of Sources

EXAMINER'S TIP

The starting point here is to be clear what Source C is saying and to identify whether the other two Sources support it. Think in terms of a short paragraph of four or five sentences. Try to conclude your answer with a point about the extent of support for Source C – what is and what is not supported.

- Source C says the Gestapo was set up to discover the enemies of the Nazi State. The statistics in Source A suggests they were successful in this – for example there were 162 734 people under 'protective arrest' in 1939. Source B supports Source C also in this respect because it agrees that discovering the enemies of the state was a prime purpose.
- Source C also says that the Gestapo used whatever means they thought necessary. This is supported by Source B which claims that the Gestapo must be able to use 'every means suited to achieve the desired ends'. Source A reveals nothing directly about this, although 'protective custody' and the use of concentration camps and execution may well fall into the category of 'whatever means'. Indeed Source C mentions these.
- Neither Source A nor Source B comments directly on the issue of whether the Gestapo instilled fear or not, but one can infer that fear of arrest, concentration camps and even death (Source A) played an important role. However, neither A nor B mentions anything directly about night-time arrests, torture and interrogation.
- So Source C's comments about the activities (in A) and role (in B) of the Gestapo is well supported by both Sources A and B.

c) Key issue: Evaluation of Sources for utility

EXAMINER'S TIP

To score well on this question you must ensure you evaluate both Sources. You need to discuss the usefulness of both Sources in terms of their content and also their nature, origin and purpose (type of source, authorship, date, audience, etc.). Do say if the Sources support each other and do point out both their strengths and limitations (by, for example, use of your own knowledge).

- Source D, as a British political cartoon, represents a comment from a British perspective on Hitler's purging of opposition within the Nazi party in the Night of the Long Knives. It should not be taken at face value as an accurate portrayal of events, but Hitler's use of brutal force to eliminate Ernst Rohm and others does indicate Hitler's ruthlessness.
- Source E is a photograph of an actual event which was typical of the use made by the Nazis of the SA to round up political opposition in 1933. Although we are not given the exact date, this photograph can be used to illustrate the treatment of the communist party after the Reichstag Fire. Of course the Communist Party, like other political parties, was prohibited later in 1933.
- So both Sources can be used to illustrate different aspects of how Hitler dealt with opposition, within and outside the Nazi Party. However, they do not provide a complete picture – opposition was also silenced by censorship and by the fear inspired by the Gestapo, for example.

d) **Key issue: Making a judgement about an interpretation which relates analysis of the Sources to wider knowledge**

EXAMINER'S TIP

This requires careful thought before an answer is written. First examine the Sources one by one to establish what they say about the way Hitler dealt with opposition. Then think about how the evidence here fits into your own knowledge of Hitler's policy towards opposition and any evidence you know about opposition to Hitler. Remember you must use both your own knowledge and the Sources to score highly.

- These Sources illustrate some of the methods used by Hitler to control opposition and to some extent demonstrate that he was successful.
- Source D, although a British cartoon, does correctly show how ruthlessly Hitler dealt with opposition from within the Nazi party and certainly illustrates his success in this respect.
- Source E, too, illustrates the methods used to eliminate other political opposition. Communists, trade union leaders, some social democrats and other political opponents were arrested and often ended up in the concentration camps.
- Source A, too, seems to show that Hitler ruthlessly suppressed opposition, by execution, protective arrest or detention in a concentration camp. The numbers involved might suggest that Hitler was successful in eliminating opposition.
- Sources C and B comment on the aims and actions of the principal instrument for seeking out and eliminating opposition – the Gestapo. However, Source B only talks of the aims and methods of the organisation. It does not comment on success. Source C asserts that the Gestapo instilled fear, and certainly many potential opponents may well have stayed quiet because of this fear.
- However, it is difficult to conclude that all opposition was totally eliminated. Source A, for instance, could indicate successful elimination, but also could be interpreted as showing the extent of opposition – the numbers are large.
- Certainly, there was little open opposition to Hitler in the 1930s after 1934 when he had made himself Führer. But there was some, for example, from some members of the Church, such as Cardinal Galen and Paul Schneider, and from unarrested members of political parties. The continued existence of the Gestapo and the intense propaganda efforts of Goebbels also suggest that the Nazis feared opposition.

Germany 1918–1945

To revise this topic more thoroughly, see Chapter 13 in *Letts GCSE History Study Guide*.

Try this sample GCSE question and then compare your answers with the Grade C and Grade A model answers on pages 95–97.

America in the 1920s

Study Sources A and B and then answer parts **a**, **b**, **c and either d or e** which follow.

Source A: Immigration statistics showing the effects of the 1921 and 1924 Immigration Acts (rounded figures are used)

Number of immigrants restricted to:	1921 3% of 1910 population	1924 2% of 1890 population
UK/Ireland	77 000	63 000
Germany/Austria	76 000	52 000
Scandinavia	42 000	19 000
Italy	43 000	4000
Eastern Europe	63 000	11 000
Russia	34 000	2000

Source B: A description of victims of Ku Klux Klan violence in Alabama, written in 1929

A black lad whipped with branches until his back was ribboned flesh, a white girl, divorcee, beaten into unconsciousness in her home; a naturalised foreigner flogged until his back was pulp because he married an American woman; a negro lashed until he sold his land to a white man for a fraction of its value.

a What can you learn from Source A about immigration into the USA in the 1920s? **[3]**
b Using Source B and your own knowledge, explain the activities of the Ku Klux Klan. **[7]**
c Describe the effects of prohibition in the USA. **[5]**

Answer **either** part **d or** part **e**

Either

d Did everyone benefit from the economic boom in the 1920s? Explain your answer. **[15]**

Or

e Why did the USA fall into Depression at the end of the 1920s? **[15]**

(AQA Paper 2 Section B Style Question: 45 minutes)

(Total 30 marks)

GRADE C ANSWER

Vicky (Vicky's answers to **b** and **d** only are shown here.)

(b) The source tells us that the Ku Klux Klan used a lot of violence against different groups — blacks, divorcees and recent immigrants. ✓ The KKK was a racist and intolerant organisation which believed in white supremacy and wanted to protect the USA from 'anti-American' influences. ✓ It used strange rituals and members paraded in white gowns and hoods. Members used coded language and had a book of rules called the Kloran.

Vicky has summarised accurately the essence of the source and added some further details about the KKK from her own knowledge. This partly helps to explain the activities of the KKK, but the last two sentences, whilst providing some interesting information, are not used effectively to help explain the activities.
4/7 marks

(d) The American economy did boom in the 1920s. There was a big boom in industries making products like cars, vacuum cleaners, radios, fridges and so on. There was also a boom in the leisure industry, especially sports like baseball and football and most of all films. ✓ Standards of living rose in America with millions being able to buy their own Model T Ford and even to buy shares on the Stock Market. ✓ The prosperity also contributed to changing lifestyles — more and more women went to work and became more independent — many were flappers who smoked and drank and went on dates. ✓ With so many people owning cars, people could move out from the city centres into suburbs and commute to work. They could also go on trips at the weekend. As a result of the boom many people became very rich and by 1928 there were over 30,000 millionaires. ✓

However, not everyone benefited from the boom. Farmers and blacks did not benefit, nor did some workers in some industries. ✓

Vicky has written quite effectively about the positive side of the boom, and clearly shows a sound understanding of many of its features and the benefits it brought. She also recognises that not everyone benefited. However, this point is not developed or explained. Overall, therefore, this is a fair but limited response.
9/15 marks

Grade booster ⤳ move a C to a B

To improve her score for **d** Vicky needed to pay more attention to those that did not benefit from the boom and explain why they did not benefit. For example, she needed to explain that agricultural prices remained very low as farms were producing too much food. The people hit hardest by this lack of possible profit were the poor sharecroppers.

To improve her answer to **b** Vicky could have picked up on the significance of Alabama – a southern and ex-slave state. She could also have developed her second sentence to explain 'anti-American' influences, by reference, for example, to the White Anglo-Saxon Protestant basis of the KKK which felt threatened not only by blacks, but by Catholics and immigrants from southern and eastern Europe who brought different languages, ideas (such as Communism) and culture with them.

USA 1919–1941

Jerome (Jerome's answers to **a**, **c** and **e** are shown here.)

(a) From Source A it is clear that the number of immigrants coming to the USA was reduced by the 1924 Act. For example, the number of immigrants coming to the USA from Scandinavia fell by over half from 42,000 to 19,000. ✓ However, it is also clear from the statistics that different areas of Europe were affected more by the 1924 Act. For example, whilst the number of immigrants from the UK, Ireland, Germany and Austria remained high, those from southern and eastern Europe fell dramatically. ✓ This was probably the intention of the Act and is indicated by the different base-line measures used to restrict immigration (1921 used 1910 figures, 1924 used 1890 figures – before the peak of immigration from southern and eastern Europe). ✓

(c) Prohibition of the sale and manufacture of alcohol was made law in the USA by the 18th Amendment to the Constitution and the Volstead Act of 1920. It had almost the opposite effect than was intended. ✓ The aim was to eliminate what was considered by many Americans to be a major cause of social problems and crime. However, once alcohol was banned demand for it seemed to increase and, being illegal, it came under the control of organised crime, gangster gangs led by colourful characters like Bugs Moran and Al Capone. ✓ In cities illegal bars ('speakeasies') opened, supplied and controlled by these gangs. The power of these gangsters was such that they could effectively control some towns and cities. ✓ Al Capone, for instance, controlled Chicago. Prohibition also increased the production of illegal and often poisonous alcohol ('moonshine') as well as encouraging profitable smuggling from Canada and Cuba. ✓

(e) There are a number of reasons for the Depression which hit the USA at the end of the 1920s. One has to do with the Wall Street Crash in October 1929 when share prices collapsed, wiping out company profits and causing many to lose fortunes. During the boom years of the 1920s companies' profits had risen and so the value of shares rose too. ✓ It seemed to many Americans that the easiest way to get rich quick was to speculate on the Stock Market by buying shares which they thought would continue to increase in value. ✓ By 1929 over 20 million Americans owned shares. Many of these were small investors who had borrowed money to buy shares 'on the margin', hoping to sell them at a profit before they need to repay the money they borrowed. This speculation inflated share prices. However, in the summer of 1929 concerns began to grow over share prices and economists began to predict a fall. It was such predictions and concerns over the economy more generally that led to the dramatic collapse on the Stock Market in October. ✓

However, the Depression was not caused by the Stock Market Crash alone. ✓ More important was the slowdown in the American economy. ✓ The farming industry had been in trouble for most of the 1920s as had many traditional industries. However, from the mid-1920s the boom in the construction industry began to decline as the demand for new buildings and roads began to fall off. The boom had been led by industries making consumer products like cars, fridges, vacuum cleaners and so on. However, by the late 1920s demand for these products began to decline. After all, once you had bought a car, fridge, radio and vacuum cleaner you did not need to buy another. ✓

American industry could not find new markets abroad, because other countries could only buy these products if the USA bought their products, but the Republican government had imposed high tariffs on imports to protect American industries.

The result of all these factors was that in 1929 the American economy went into a depression. Firms laid off workers who could not then afford to buy products and so profits fell further and firms were forced to close. ✓

USA 1919–1941

Grade booster ····> move A to A*

In his answer to e Jerome has missed a major element in explaining the Depression – the banking crisis – and could have explained its role. He could also give a little detail to support his point about American tariffs by giving an example of tariff legislation. He could also explain a little more carefully in his conclusion how each of the chosen factors linked to the others.

1 Answer all the questions a), b) and c) which follow on the Depression in the USA.

a) What were the main features of the Depression after 1929? (4)

b) Explain why the Wall Street Stock Market crashed in October 1929. (6)

c) 'The most important reason why Herbert Hoover lost the 1932 presidential election was his failure to do anything to help America out of Depression.' Do you agree with this statement? Explain your answer. (10)

(OCR Paper 1, Section B Style Question: 35 minutes)

TOTAL 20

2 This question is about President Roosevelt and the New Deal. Look carefully at Sources A to F and then answer questions a) to d) which follow.

Source A: Roosevelt's promise to the American people from a pre-election speech made in 1932

Millions of our citizens cherish the hope that their old standards of living have not gone forever. Those millions shall not hope in vain. I pledge you, I pledge myself to a New Deal for the American people.

Source B: A cartoon, published in March 1933, showing President Roosevelt throwing out the policies of the previous government

Source C: An extract from *The New York Times*, June 1936. *The New York Times* supported the Republican Party

The New Deal administration has been guilty of a frightful waste and extravagance. It has created a vast number of new offices and sent out swarms of inspectors to harass our people. It has destroyed the morale of many of our people and made them dependent on the government.

Source D: The table below shows the numbers of unemployed in the USA

Unemployment in the USA, 1929–1942

Source E: A modern historian here assesses the success of the New Deal

If the New Deal is judged by economic success alone, then the verdict must be a mixed one. But, generally speaking, the economy had by 1937 recovered to the level reached before the Depression started in 1929. The New Deal also established a far more important role for the Federal government in a whole range of areas. Roosevelt deliberately extended the powers of central government in order to achieve a fairer society and offer its citizens greater security.

Source F: A modern historian gives his conclusion on the success of the New Deal

The most damning criticism of Roosevelt's policy was that it failed to cure the Depression. Despite some $20 billion poured out in spending and lending, there were still millions of dispirited men unemployed.

a) Study Source A. What can you learn from Source A about Roosevelt and the New Deal? ④

b) Study Sources A, B and C. Do Sources B and C support the evidence of Source A? Explain your answer. ⑥

c) Study Sources D and E. How useful are these two Sources as evidence about the success of the New Deal? ⑧

d) Study all the Sources. Source F suggests that the New Deal 'failed to cure the Depression'. Use these Sources, and your own knowledge, to explain whether you agree that the New Deal was a failure. ⑫

(Edexcel Paper 2 Style Question: 50 minutes)

TOTAL 30

3 This question would be part of a larger question about change in the USA, 1929–1990

Information: In 1929 America was hit by depression and the numbers of unemployed rose to over 12 million. In 1932 President Roosevelt was elected and instituted the New Deal.

a) What was the Wall Street Crash? ②

b) Describe how the New Deal aimed to solve the problem of unemployment. ④

(WJEC Style Question)

TOTAL 6

1 a)   Key issue: Knowledge of a key event

EXAMINER'S TIP

> *Highlight and give some detail of a few key features in a short paragraph.*

- Unemployment; by 1933 over 12 million Americans were out of work.
- Many banks were forced to close, in 1929 over 650 banks failed.
- International trade collapsed, by 1933 it was a third of what it had been in 1929.
- Industrial production fell by 40% between 1928 and 1933.

b)   Key issue: Explanation of a key event

EXAMINER'S TIP

> *The emphasis here is on giving reasons and supporting them with evidence. Think of three points to follow 'The Wall Street Crash happened because …'.*

- Because in October 1929 investors lost confidence that share prices would continue to rise and decided to sell. This led to a collapse in share prices as everyone wanted to sell and few wanted to buy.
- Because by the summer of 1929 share prices were unrealistically high. Speculators had assumed that share prices would continue to rise and this had pushed up prices beyond the true value of the industry they related to.
- Because by the summer of 1929 the American economy was already slowing down with company profits falling and production being cut. This undermined confidence in the Stock Market leading to the panic selling of October.

c)   Key issue: Assessment of the reasons for a key event

EXAMINER'S TIP

> *The key here is to make sure you deal with both Hoover's responsibility for his own defeat and other factors and so come to a balanced judgement.*

- It is certainly true that Hoover appeared to do little to try and solve the problems caused by the Depression. He was known as a 'do nothing' president and his name became closely associated with the worst effects of the slump – the Hoovervilles or shanty towns of unemployed and homeless that grew up on wasteland in towns and cities.
- However, it is not entirely true that he made no effort to solve the Depression. In 1930 and 1931 he reduced taxes, he tried to persuade businesses not to cut wages and instituted the Reconstruction Finance Company to support banks. He also increased tariffs on foreign goods to try and protect US firms.
- Yet all these measures were little more than tinkering at a time when more radical measures were required. This was partly because Hoover believed that booms and slumps were a necessary feature of the economic cycle and so he remained convinced the 'prosperity was just around the corner'.
- More significantly in electoral terms Hoover did little to help the poor and desperate. He believed it was wrong for the Government to issue relief. This was a matter for local government and charity. When thousands of servicemen marched to Washington in 1932 to ask for their war bonuses to be paid early, the Government's answer was tear gas and the burning of the marchers' camps.
- On the other hand, if there had not been a real alternative to Hoover then perhaps the result of the 1932 election might not have been so clear-cut. In Roosevelt the electorate had a real alternative to the 'do nothing' president. Roosevelt promised action when Hoover offered nothing. He wanted government to be active in helping people and to spend money to get people back to work. He promised a 'New Deal' for the American people and a war on despair. After three years of extreme and increasing hardship Roosevelt's message, however vague, offered hope and a way out. He won by a landslide.
- Whilst Hoover did much to bring about his own defeat, the election came after three years of deepening depression. His policies, such as they were, hadn't worked and he seemed indifferent to people's suffering. Roosevelt offered something different and the result of the election was perhaps a foregone conclusion. It can be forcefully argued that in many ways Hoover did bring about his own defeat.

a) Key issue: Understanding of Source

EXAMINER'S TIP

Keep points brief and to the point. Try to draw any inferences you can.

- The Source gives evidence of the promises made by Roosevelt in the election campaign. He was offering a New Deal – a change of policy from the Republicans under Hoover.
- The American people had been suffering due to the Depression. Roosevelt was promising a return to the standards of living enjoyed in the '20s boom years.
- We can infer from this that Roosevelt was an able politician, tapping into the hopes and fears of the electorate to win support. The promises are vague and lack detail, but offer a clear alternative to the Republicans.

b) Key issue: Comparison of Sources to establish corroboration

EXAMINER'S TIP

Start with the evidence of Source A then say how far each or both of the Sources B and C support it.

- In Source A Roosevelt offered the American people hope and a New Deal – a different policy from the Republicans.
- This is supported by Source B which shows Roosevelt throwing out the failed policies of the previous administration once he came to office. It offers direct evidence that in this respect Roosevelt was fulfilling his promise to the American people.
- Source A is not so well supported by Source C. Although Roosevelt is clearly pursuing new policies and there is reference to the 'New Deal administration' as promised, these policies, according to Source C, far from fulfilling people's hopes, are destroying their morale and their independence.
- So both Sources B and C support Source A in so far as Roosevelt, once in power, rejected Republican policies and instated a New Deal. However, Source C criticises the New Deal – criticism to be expected from a Republican newspaper.

c) Key issue: Assessment of the usefulness of Sources

EXAMINER'S TIP

Refer to content and the nature, origin and purpose of the Source in your answer. Also use your own knowledge where relevant. Try to assess whether one Source is more useful than the other, or whether they are most useful when taken together.

- The acid test of the success of the New Deal, for many Americans, would be how far it reduced unemployment. The statistics in Source D, therefore, are very useful in assessing the degree of success in this respect. They show that unemployment fell from 14 million in 1933 to 6 million in 1941.
- However, we cannot tell from these statistics what was responsible for the fall in unemployment. It could, for example, have been due to a general upturn in the economy.
- Interestingly the figures show that unemployment rose in 1938, to fall again as war approached in 1941. Some argue the war was really responsible for solving unemployment.
- Source E represents the judgement of an historian who has studied the period, and is based on his reading of the evidence. We are not told whether he has any particular sympathies, but he does use evidence to back up his judgements.
- It treats the New Deal as a whole, judging it to be a mixed success – economic activity only recovered to 1929 levels in 1937.
- The Source also highlights other aims of the New Deal – Roosevelt intended to achieve a fairer society and offer American citizens greater security. However, no judgement is made here as to success.
- Taken together, both Sources are quite useful in assessing the New Deal. Source D supports the judgement in Source E that in economic terms it had some but not total success. However, although Source D refers to other aims of the New Deal it offers no useful evidence to assess success in those aims.

d) Key issue: Using Sources and own knowledge to reach a judgement

EXAMINER'S TIP

The most important thing here is to ensure that you do use the Sources and your own knowledge. Try to plan carefully – evidence for and against. This will help you come to a balanced conclusion.

- There is evidence in the Sources that the New Deal can be considered a failure. Source F quotes expenditure of $20 billion by the Government but the persistence of high unemployment. This point can be supported by the unemployment statistics given in Source D. They show that there were still 8 million unemployed in 1937 and that this rose to over 10 million in 1938.

The notion that expenditure was wasteful is also reinforced in Source C, which highlights the growth of bureaucracy and red tape as a result of the New Deal. Source C also supports Source F in the claim that rather than inspiring people with hope, the New Deal undermined morale and produced dispirited unemployed.

- Certainly the New Deal came in for a good deal of criticism from Republicans and many businessmen. It also fell foul of the Supreme Court which was dominated by Republicans. Others, like Huey Long, criticised the New Deal for not doing enough.
- Some people did not benefit from the job creation schemes of the New Deal. Black people, for example, benefited less than whites – in 1935 about a third of black people were dependent on relief payments.
- However, whilst it is true that the New Deal did not achieve as much as many had hoped it was not a failure. As Source D demonstrates, unemployment did fall, at least in part, because of the New Deal, from 14 million to just 8 million. Unemployment rose again only because the Government reduced New Deal spending in 1938. Source E also acknowledges that the New Deal helped revive economic activity to pre-Depression levels by 1937.
- Schemes like the TVA brought lasting economic benefits to the USA, whilst alphabet agencies like the CWA, PWA, WPA and the AAA brought much needed work and support for millions of Americans.
- Source E also comments on the work the New Deal did to make the USA a fairer society and it did provide relief for those at the bottom of society. As important, perhaps, was the hope it gave the Americans at a time of despair, as Source A suggests.
- Certainly the American people as a whole believed that the New Deal was a good thing. That is why Roosevelt was re-elected by a landslide in 1936 (only two states out of 48 voted against him).
- The New Deal was not a failure, but neither was it a total success. Source E seems most appropriate as a summary – the verdict must be 'a mixed one'.

❸a) Key issue: Understanding of a term

EXAMINER'S TIP

Be brief and precise.

- The Wall Street Crash refers to the collapse in share prices on New York's Stock Exchange that occurred in October 1929 and started the American Depression.

b) Key issue: Description of key features of an event

EXAMINER'S TIP

You need to stick to the main points and give accurate evidence to support them.

- The basic way the New Deal hoped to solve unemployment was by the Government putting money into the economy to provide new jobs.
- It did this through a number of schemes. For example, the Civil Works Administration employed unemployed Americans on a range of public works, from sweeping in public parks to building roads. Four million temporary jobs were created.
- There were also the Public Works Administration and the Works Progress Administration which provided long-term and local work schemes to get the unemployed back to work.
- The millions of Americans who got jobs through these agencies then received wages that they could spend on goods and services. This in turn helped businesses which now needed to employ more people because of the upturn in their trade.

Centre number	
Candidate number	
Surname and initials	

 **Examining Group**

General Certificate of Secondary Education

History
Paper 1

For Examiner's use only	
1	
2	
3	
4	
5	
6	
7	
Total	

Time: 1 hour 45 minutes

Instructions to candidates

The following exam is based on the AQA specification and deals with the most popular options. The questions cover topics which are also popular with the other examination boards.

Answer three questions, including two from Section A and one from Section B

You are advised to spend 70 minutes on Section A and 35 minutes on Section B.

EDUCATIONAL

SECTION A Answer two questions only

1 **The Treaty of Versailles and Germany**
Study Sources A and B and then answer the following questions.

Source A: Lloyd George, British Prime Minister speaking in early 1919 to Parliament before the Paris Peace Conference
We want a peace which will be just, but not vindictive. We want a stern peace because the occasion demands it, but the severity must be designed, not for vengeance, but for justice.

Source B: Extract from the *Deutsche Zeitung* (German News) on the day the Treaty of Versailles was signed
Today in the Hall of Mirrors the disgraceful Treaty is being signed. Do not forget it! The German people will, with unceasing labour, press forward to reconquer the place among the nations to which it is entitled.

(a) According to Source A, what was the British view of the peace treaty that should be made with Germany? **[3]**

(b) Source B refers to the Treaty of Versailles with Germany. Describe the main terms of this treaty. **[6]**

(c) How useful is Source B to an historian writing about German reactions to the Treaty of Versailles? Use Source B and your own knowledge to explain your answer. **[6]**

(d) Which of the Big Three had most influence on the Treaty of Versailles? Explain your answer. **[10]**

(Total 25 marks)

2 **Hitler, Appeasement and the outbreak of the Second World War**
Study Sources C and D and answer the questions which follow.

Source C: Albert Speer, a prominent Nazi, remembers Hitler's view of the re-militarisation of the Rhineland in 1936
Even later, when Hitler was waging war against almost the entire world, he always termed the re-militarisation of the Rhineland the most daring of all his undertakings. 'We had no army worth mentioning. If the French had taken any action, we would have been easily defeated: our resistance would have been over in a few days.'

Source D: Speaking in Parliament in October 1938, Clement Atlee, leader of the Labour Party gives his reaction to the agreements about Czechoslovakia reached at Munich
The events of the last few days are one of the greatest diplomatic defeats this country and France have ever suffered. There can be no doubt that it is a tremendous victory for Herr Hitler. Without firing a shot, he has achieved a dominating position in Europe.

(a) According to Source C, what was Hitler's view of the re-militarisation of the Rhineland by German forces in 1936? **[3]**

(b) Source D refers to the agreements made at the Munich Conference in September 1938. Describe what happened at the Munich Conference. **[6]**

(c) How reliable is Source D to an historian writing about British reactions to the results of the Munich Conference? Use Source D and your own knowledge to explain your answer. **[6]**

(d) Was appeasement the most important reason for the outbreak of the Second World War? Explain your answer. **[10]**

(Total 25 marks)

104

3 The Development of the Cold War 1945–1949

Source E: Stalin speaking about Poland in February 1945
Mr Churchill has said that for Great Britain the Polish question is one of honour.
But for the Russians it is a question both of honour and security. Throughout
history Poland has been the corridor for attack on Russia. It is not merely a
question of honour for Russia, but one of life and death.

Source F: A British cartoon from March 1946 commenting on the Iron Curtain between East and West

Peep under the Iron Curtain

(a) According to Source E, why was the future of Poland so important to
Stalin? **[3]**

(b) Source F refers to the way the Iron Curtain divided Europe. Describe how
Europe had become divided at the end of the Second World War. **[6]**

(c) How useful is Source F to an historian writing about what happened in
Europe after the defeat of Hitler's Germany? Use Source F and your own
knowledge to explain your answer. **[6]**

(d) Why did the rivalry between the USA and the USSR increase in the period
1945–49? Explain your answer. **[10]**

(Total 25 marks)

4 Czechoslovakia and Détente

**Source G: The Brezhnev Doctrine, issued by the Soviet leader justifying
Soviet intervention in Czechoslovakia in 1968**
When internal and external forces hostile to socialism attempt to turn the
development of any communist country in the direction of the capitalist system,
when a threat arises to the cause of communism in that country, it becomes not
only a problem for the people of that country but also a general problem, the
concern of all communist countries.

[turn over

Source H: Photograph of President Nixon of the USA meeting President Brezhnev of the Soviet Union in 1974

(a) According to Source G, what was the Soviet justification for intervening in Czechoslovakia in 1968? **[3]**

(b) How useful is Source H to an historian writing about Détente in the 1970s? Use Source H and your own knowledge to explain your answer. **[6]**

(c) Describe the main features of the Strategic Arms Limitation Treaty (SALT 1) and the Helsinki Agreement. **[6]**

(d) Was the Soviet invasion of Afghanistan the most important reason for the collapse of Détente and renewal of Cold War in the late 1970s and early 1980s? Explain your answer. **[10]**

(Total 25 marks)

5 **The collapse of Communism**

Source I: Gennadi Gerasimov, Soviet government spokesman, speaking in October 1989
The Brezhnev Doctrine is dead. You know the Frank Sinatra song 'My Way'? Hungary and Poland are doing it their way. We now have the Sinatra Doctrine. So Hungary, Poland and other countries have it their own way. They decide which road to take. It's their business.

(a) According to Source I, what were the results of the Soviet Union dropping the Brezhnev Doctrine? **[3]**

(b) How reliable is Source I to an historian writing about Soviet policies towards Eastern Europe at the end of the 1980s? Use Source I and your own knowledge to explain your answer. **[6]**

(c) Describe Gorbachev's policies of Glasnost and Perestroika. **[6]**

(d) Was Gorbachev the most important reason for the collapse of communist control in Eastern Europe at the end of the 1980s? Explain your answer. **[10]**

(Total 25 marks)

6   Britain in the First World War

Study Sources A, B, C and D and then answer all parts of Question 6 which follow.

Source A: Women delivering coal in 1917

Source B: A 1915 recruitment poster

Source C: Prime Minister Lloyd George in a private conversation with the editor of the *Manchester Guardian* in December 1917 said:

If the people really knew the truth about the war, it would be stopped tomorrow. But of course they don't – and can't – know. The journalists don't write, and the censors would not pass, the truth.

Source D: Measures taken to deal with food shortages described in a modern school textbook

Shortage of food caused by the German U-boat blockade was addressed by additional laws through DORA (the Defence of the Realm Act). Public parks were taken over for the growing of vegetables, the Women's Land Army was set up and posters were produced to encourage people to support the country by reducing the amount of food they had at meal times. Even feeding bread to pigeons was forbidden.

(a) What does Source A tell us about the contribution of women to the war effort?   **[3]**

(b) How useful is Source B to an historian studying why people volunteered for the army in 1914 and 1915? Use Source B and your own knowledge to answer the question.   **[8]**

(c) Using Source C and your own knowledge, explain why the Government wanted to control or censor information during the First World War.   **[6]**

(d) 'The German U-boat campaign came very close to starving Britain into submission.' Is this a fair interpretation? Use Source D and your own knowledge to answer the question.   **[8]**

(Total 25 marks)

     [turn over

Letts

7 Britain in the Second World War

Study Sources A, B, C and D and then answer all parts of Question 7 which follow.

Source A: A Government minister comments on the impact of bombing during the Blitz in his diary 17 September 1940
Everybody is worried about the feeling in the East End (of London), where there is much bitterness. It is said that even the King and Queen were booed the other day when they visited the destroyed areas.

Source B: A propaganda poster to recruit women workers during the war

Source C: Coping with problems of food supply
Since it was difficult to import food, efforts were made to grow more. Cartoon characters such as 'Dr Carrot' called on people to 'Dig for Victory'. Even the Tower of London's moat was turned into allotments. To release farmworkers for the armed services and to help grow more food, over 40,000 women joined the Women's Land Army, and they were chiefly responsible for a near doubling of the food supply by 1944.

Source D: Winston Churchill speaking in the House of Commons, 4 June 1940
We shall defend our island, whatever the cost may be. We shall fight on the beaches, we shall fight on the landing grounds, we shall fight in the fields and in the streets, we shall fight in the hills. We shall never surrender.

(a) What does Source A suggest about people's attitudes towards German bombing during the Blitz? **[3]**

(b) How useful is Source B to an historian studying the role of women in Britain during the Second World War? Use Source B and your own knowledge to answer the question. **[8]**

(c) Using Source C and your own knowledge, how well did Britain cope with the problems of food supply during the Second World War? **[6]**

(d) 'Churchill's leadership was vital for maintaining the British war effort.' Is this a fair interpretation? Use Source D and your own knowledge to answer the question. **[8]**

(Total 25 marks)

Letts

| Centre number |
| Candidate number |
| Surname and initials |

 **Examining Group**

General Certificate of Secondary Education

History
Paper 2

Time: 1 hour 45 minutes

Instructions to candidates

The following exam is based on AQA specification and deals with the most popular options. The questions cover topics which are also popular with other examination boards.

Answer two questions, including one from Section A and one from Section B. Each question answered must be answered on a different country.

You are advised to spend 1 hour on Section A and 45 minutes on Section B.

You are strongly advised to read all the questions on your chosen countries in both Sections before deciding which questions to answer.

EDUCATIONAL

1   **Germany – The Rise of Hitler**

Study Sources A to D and then answer all parts of the question.

Source A: The Reichstag Election results 1928–1932 (number of seats won by major parties)

Party	May 1928	Sept 1930	July 1932	Nov 1932	March 1933
Right Wing					
Nazis	12	107	230	196	288
Nationalists	73	41	37	52	52
Centre					
People's Party	45	30	7	11	2
Centre	62	68	75	70	74
Democrats	25	20	4	2	5
Left Wing					
Social Democrats	153	143	133	121	120
Communists	54	77	89	100	81

Source B: The headmistress of a girls' school explains why she supported the Nazis in the early 1930s

I saw the communist danger, their gangs breaking up middle class meetings, the middle class parties being utterly helpless, the Nazis being the only party that broke terror with anti-terror. I saw the complete failure of the middle class parties to deal with the economic crisis. Only National Socialism offered any hope.

Source C: A Nazi election poster from 1932. The slogan is 'Our Last Hope: Hitler!'

Source D: A cartoon commenting on the elections to the Reichstag on 5 March 1933 published in the *Daily Express*, a British newspaper

(a) Explain what you can learn from Source A about Hitler's rise to power in the years 1928–1933. **[5]**

(b) Do Sources B and C agree about the reasons why people supported the Nazis? **[6]**

(c) How useful is source B for learning about Hitler's success in the elections between 1928 and 1933? Explain your answer using Source B and your own knowledge. **[9]**

(d) Is Source D an accurate interpretation of why the Nazis won the March 1933 election?
Use Source D and your own knowledge to answer the question. **[10]**

(e) Use your own knowledge to explain how Hitler made himself a dictator in Germany between 1933 and 1934. **[15]**

(Total 45 marks)

2 USA – 1920s

Study Sources A to E and then answer all parts of the question.

Source A: The initiation of a new member into the Ku Klux Klan at a Klan ceremony in November 1922

[turn over

Letts

Source B: Extracts from the Kloran, the Ku Klux Klan's book of rules, listing questions prospective members had to answer yes to

Are you a native-born, white, non-Jewish American?
Do you believe in the Christian religion?
Will you faithfully strive for the eternal maintenance of white supremacy?

Source C: A newspaper account of the lynching of a black man accused of killing a white woman in Georgia in 1921. The story was published in the *Washington Eagle*

The Negro was chained to a tree stump by over 500 Klan members and asked if he had anything to say. Castrated and in indescribable agony, the Negro asked for a cigarette, lit it, and blew smoke in the face of the Klan members. The fire was lit and everyone danced around.

Source D: An extract from the Chicago Property Owners' Journal, 1920

There is nothing in the make up of a Negro, physically or mentally, that should induce anyone to welcome him as a neighbour. The best of them are unsanitary. Ruin follows in their path. They are as proud as peacocks, but have nothing of the peacock's beauty. Niggers are undesirable neighbours and entirely irresponsible and full of vice.

Source E: An interpretation of growth of the Ku Klux Klan in the 1920s by a modern historian

The Klan's greatest selling point was the protection of traditional American values. These were to be found in the bosoms and communities of white, native-born, Anglo-Saxon, Protestants. The changing world of the 1920s, which saw post-war restlessness and new waves of immigration combined with the erosion of both the small town and traditional morality, brought the Klan millions of recruits.

(a) Explain what you can learn from Source A about the Ku Klux Klan. **[5]**

(b) Compare Source B and Source C. Are they agreeing about who the Klan were opposed to? **[6]**

(c) How useful is Source D as evidence about racial attitudes in the USA in the 1920s?
Explain your answer using Source D and your own knowledge. **[9]**

(d) How accurate an interpretation is Source E of why the Ku Klux Klan won support in the 1920s? Explain your answer by using Source E and your own knowledge. **[10]**

(e) The 1920s in the USA are sometimes called the 'Boom Years'. Use your own knowledge to explain the extent to which this was the case. **[15]**

(Total 45 marks)

3   Germany – Hitler in power

Study Sources A and B and then answers parts **(a)**, **(b)**, **(c)** and either **(d)** or **(e)**.

Source A: The daily timetable for a girls' school in Nazi Germany

School day starts at 8 am	
Period 1	German (every day)
Period 2	Geography or history or singing
Period 3	Race Studies and Ideology
Break	(Special announcements, Sports)
Period 4	Domestic Science or Maths
Period 5	Eugenics or Health Biology
Lunch	
Afternoon (2 pm – 6 pm)	Sport
Evening	Sex education or Ideology or Domestic Science

Source B: Hitler outlines his views on young people
In my great educative work I am beginning with the young. With them I can make a new world.
My teaching is hard. Weakness has to be knocked out of them. A violently active, dominating, fearless and brutal youth – that is what I am after. It must be indifferent to pain. There must be no tenderness in it.
I will have no intellectual training. Knowledge is ruin to my young men.

(a) What can you learn from Source A about the education of young people in Nazi Germany?   **[3]**

(b) Using Source B and your own knowledge, explain what Hitler aimed to achieve with his policies for young people.   **[7]**

(c) Describe Nazi policies towards women.   **[5]**

Answer **either** part **(d)** or part **(e)**.

Either

(d) How successful were Nazi economic policies? Explain your answer.   **[15]**

Or

(e) How successful were the Nazis in eliminating all opposition in Germany after 1933? Explain your answer.   **[15]**

(**Total 30 marks**)

[turn over

4 USA – The Wall Street Crash and Roosevelt's New Deal

Study Sources A and B and then answer parts **(a)**, **(b)**, **(c)** and either **(d)** or **(e)**.

Source A: An American who witnessed the Depression wrote this account
One vivid, gruesome moment of those dark days we shall never forget. We saw a crowd of some fifty men fighting over a barrel of garbage outside the back door of a restaurant. American citizens fighting for scraps of food like animals.

Source B: A cartoon published by opponents of the New Deal. It shows Roosevelt 'priming the pump' with money

(a) What can you learn from Source A about the effects of the Depression in the USA?   **[3]**

(b) Using Source B and your own knowledge, explain why the New Deal was criticised by some Americans.   **[7]**

(c) Describe what Roosevelt did during the Hundred Days.   **[5]**

Answer **either** part **(d)** or part **(e)**

Either

(d) Did all Americans benefit from the New Deal? Explain your answer.   **[15]**

Or

(e) Why were the consequences of the Wall Street Crash so serious?   **[15]**

(Total 30 marks)

Answers to mock examination Paper 1

1 (a) Key issue: Understanding a Source

- Britain wanted a harsh peace, because Germany deserved it.
- The peace must also be 'just' or fair, not vengeful.

(b) Key issue: Knowledge and understanding of a key event

- Germany was blamed for starting the war in the War Guilt Clause.
- Germany's armed forces were restricted, for example only 100 000 men and no tanks. Germany lost territory, for example, all her colonies and West Prussia (given to Poland).
- The Rhineland was de-militarised and Alsace-Lorraine returned to France.
- Germany was to pay reparations to the allies for the damage they caused.
- Anschluss or union with Austria was forbidden.

(c) Key issue: Evaluation of utility using own knowledge

- Source B suggests that German reaction was one of disgust – the Treaty is described as 'disgraceful'.
- Source B also suggests that the German people will want to overturn the Treaty and 'reconquer' their place amongst the nations.
- Source B is from a German newspaper of the time and so can be taken to reflect the views of its readers. Because of this what it says about German attitudes is likely to be fairly reliable and typical.
- The views expressed fit in with what is known about German reactions but does not give a complete picture of why the Germans felt so bitter about the Treaty.
- Most Germans believed the Treaty to be unjust, a peace of vengeance and not based on Wilson's 14 points as they had expected. Many resented the idea it blamed Germany alone for the war (War Guilt Clause) and the loss of German land to Poland was

also deeply resented. What is more the peace treaty was resented as a Diktat which Germany was forced to sign or face invasion.

- So Source B is useful as a general indication of German views, but does not give a complete picture.

(d) Key issue: Understanding of a key event

- The Big Three were Clemenceau of France, Lloyd George of Britain and Wilson of the USA. They agreed on much – such as the War Guilt Clause and the return of Alsace-Lorraine to France.
- Wilson probably had least influence. However, he did ensure that clauses relating to the League of Nations were included and exercised a moderating influence on the ambitions of France.
- Britain also tried to moderate French aims as she did not want to see Germany destroyed as an economic power. She also wanted, however, to ensure Germany's naval power was destroyed and this was reflected in the Treaty.
- France, however, had the most influence. After all she had borne the brunt of the war and wanted to ensure Germany could never threaten her again. France was pleased with clauses which destroyed Germany's armed forces and took away lands from her – in particular Alsace-Lorraine.
- However, France did not get all her own way. Reparations, although high, were not as high as she wanted. Although the Rhineland was de-militarised, France would have preferred the creation of a separate buffer state.
- So, although all had an influence, France probably had the greatest.

Marking

2 (a) Key issue: Understanding of Source

- It was a great risk – the greatest risk Hitler ever took.
- If the French had resisted Hitler would have been defeated.

Marking

(b) Key issue: Knowledge and understanding of a key event

- The Munich conference was attended by Germany, France, Britain and Italy. Czechoslovakia and the USSR were not invited.
- It met to discuss the fate of Czechoslovakia and the Sudetenland in particular.
- Britain and France agreed that Hitler could take over the Sudetenland in October. They would not support Czechoslovakia if she resisted.
- Britain and Germany agreed the so-called Munich Agreement, a piece of paper on which Chamberlain (British Prime Minister) and Hitler agreed that there were no reasons for Britain and Germany to go to war. Chamberlain said that it guaranteed 'peace for our time'.
- It was the final time Britain and France 'appeased' Hitler.

Marking

(c) Key issue: Evaluation of the reliability of a Source in context

- Source D claimed Munich was a 'diplomatic defeat', but a huge victory for Hitler. Germany was now the master of central Europe.
- It is taken from a speech in Parliament in which he is stating his view but may also be seeking to persuade others of it.
- This view is that of the leader of the Labour Party and therefore reflects that of his party. Churchill and a few other politicians had a similar view. The

source is therefore a reliable indicator of some people's views.

- However, it is not necessarily a reliable indicator of the views of all British people.
- Chamberlain was hailed as a hero by the British press on his return from Munich. He was the person who had saved Britain from war and guaranteed 'peace for our time'.
- Source D therefore, whilst reliable as a reaction to the Conference, should not be taken as typical of the British people as a whole or of even the majority of British people.

Marking

(d) Key issue: Evaluation of the reasons for a key historical event

- Appeasement was one of a number of reasons for WW2. Others include: long-term causes like the impact of the peace treaties after WW1, the effects of the Great Depression and the failure of the League of Nations; short-term causes like the aggressive policies of Hitler and immediate causes like the Nazi–Soviet Pact.
- Appeasement means giving into the 'reasonable' demands of aggressive powers in order to avoid war. It was a policy actively pursued by the British Prime Minister Chamberlain in the late 1930s, for example, at Munich.
- Appeasement is important in explaining the outbreak of war because it encouraged Hitler and other aggressive powers to believe that whatever they demanded they would get because neither Britain nor France would resist them. This was the lesson that Hitler drew from Chamberlain's agreement at Munich. It encouraged Hitler to believe that Britain and France would not do anything when he occupied the rest of Czechoslovakia in March 1939 or Poland in September 1939. Russia might have prevented the latter invasion had not Stalin signed the Nazi–Soviet pact in August 1939 which gave Hitler the green light to attack.
- However, Appeasement did not cause WW2 on its own. If Hitler (and Japan and Italy) had not pursued aggressive foreign policies in the 1930s, war would not have occurred. Hitler wanted to undo the Treaty of Versailles and talked of creating a Greater Germany and conquering 'Lebensraum' or living space. He had prepared for war with Czechoslovakia in 1938 and had been 'cheated' of it by appeasement.

- Hitler would not have come to power were it not for the combined effects of the Treaty of Versailles and the Great Depression. Mussolini would not have come to power if Italy had won suitable rewards at the end of WW1, and Japan pursued her aggressive policies against China as a way out of the effects of the Depression.
- All these reasons therefore combine to explain why war broke out in 1939. If one was more important than the others, it was not Appeasement, which was a reaction to aggression, but Hitler's actions without which Appeasement would not have been necessary. Appeasement may have encouraged Hitler, but arguably it delayed the outbreak of war by giving in to aggression, rather than brought it about.

3 (a) Key issue: Understanding of Source

- Source F suggests that Poland is so important for the Soviet Union for two reasons:
  - honour
  - security.
- The latter is most important because having a friendly government in Poland is a matter of life and death for Russia.

(b) Key issue: Knowledge and understanding of a key development

- The division of Europe at the end of the Second World War largely reflected the areas occupied or liberated by the western allies on the one hand and the Soviet Union on the other.
- The Red Army had occupied Poland, Eastern Germany, Czechoslovakia, parts of Austria and most of the Balkan states. The Soviet Union wanted to ensure there would be friendly, i.e. Communist, governments in these states.
- What to do about post-war Europe was discussed at two major conferences at Yalta and Potsdam. The main discussions concerned the future of Poland and Germany.
- Whatever the agreements about 'free elections', however, the presence of the Red Army was the decisive argument on the future of Eastern Europe.
- By 1948 Poland, Czechoslovakia, Hungary, Romania and Bulgaria had pro-Soviet governments. Eastern Germany would go the same way after the Berlin blockade in 1949.

(c) Key issue: Evaluation of utility of a Source

- The cartoon shows divided Europe, with the Soviet controlled east protected from Western sight by an Iron Curtain. The British Prime Minister is trying to see what is happening by looking under the curtain.
- This source is useful to a degree in that it reflects what happened in Europe at the end of the war. Soviet forces occupied Eastern Europe and ensured friendly governments there.
- However, this is a cartoon in a British newspaper and therefore reflects a Western viewpoint. It was drawn soon after Winston Churchill's famous 'Iron Curtain' speech in America.
- The Source therefore is useful as a visual representation of the Western view of what happened in Europe at the end of the war, but does not tell us the Soviet viewpoint.

(d) Key issue: Explanation of causation

- The period 1945–49 saw the development of the Cold War in Europe. The period began with the tensions that emerged over what should happen in Europe once Hitler had been defeated and ended with the Berlin Blockade, the formation of NATO and the setting up of separate West and East German states.
- One reason rivalry grew in this period was the ideological difference between the USA and the USSR. The USA believed in capitalism and democracy, whilst the USSR believed in communism. These ideologies were opposed to each other. The wartime alliance had merely papered over these differences whilst the common enemy of Nazism was defeated.
- The tension which grew steadily emerged first at Yalta over Poland and then at Potsdam over Germany.
- It quickly became apparent to the West that the Soviet Union wanted to ensure friendly (and therefore communist) states on its borders and the

West feared that the Soviet Union wanted to spread communism further still. Something of the division was reflected in the Iron Curtain speech made by Winston Churchill in 1946.

- When Greece was threatened with a communist takeover the USA issued the Truman Doctrine (1947) which promised support to anti-communist forces. This was backed up with the offer of Marshall Aid – financial and economic help – to get war-torn economies back on their feet. It was felt that if economies recovered the appeal of communism would be lessened. The USSR interpreted these moves as US imperialism in action, and formed Comecon to coordinate the Eastern bloc economies. So tension increased.

- By 1948 tensions were running high and were made worse by the communist takeover of Czechoslovakia in that year and disagreements over the future of Germany. The disagreements culminated in the Berlin blockade and the subsequent airlift. The result of this was the drawing of the final battle lines between East and West in Europe with the creation of separate East and West German states.

Marking

Either: Simple answer of one cause, based on a single reason
Or: A generalised answer suggesting that there were many causes. **[1–2]**
Either: Picks one cause and justifies the choice without discussing others
Or: Mentions several causes without effective argument. **[3–5]**
Discusses at least two causes with argument. **[6–8]**
A sustained and detailed multicausal answer, relevant to the question. **[9–10]**

4 (a) Key issue: Understanding of Source
- The Source says that a threat to communism in any one communist state is a threat to all communist states and therefore other communist states are justified in intervening to quash the threat.

Marking

Give up to two marks for one relevant point made depending on development, and three marks for two relevant points made. **[1–3]**

(b) Key issue: Evaluation of utility of a Source in context
- Source shows a meeting between the American and Soviet leaders in 1974. This kind of summit was typical of the era of détente and so the Source provides a useful example of this. The first summit occurred in 1972 and there were a further four during the 1970s.
- The body language of the two leaders is open and friendly and this indicates the improved relations that occurred during the 1970s.
- However, this photograph can tell us little more about détente. It does not, for example, provide any evidence of the measures which reflected détente – such as the Strategic Arms Limitation Treaty (SALT 1).

- Nor does the Source indicate the reasons for détente, such as the desire to reduce the risk of nuclear war, the American desire to improve relations after its defeat in the Vietnam War and mutual concerns over developments in the Middle East.

Marking

Basic description, e.g. 'Shows the two leaders shaking hands'. **[1–2]**
Either: Some detailed description
Or: A wide range of points without explanation. **[3–4]**
Detailed description of strengths and limitations. **[5–6]**

(c) Key Issue: Understanding of an event
- Talks began about limiting strategic arms in 1969 and SALT 1 in 1972 was the result of these negotiations.
- Under the terms of the Strategic Arms Limitation Treaty both sides agreed to reductions in their anti-ballistic missile systems and limits on the number of their offensive missiles and bombers.
- Reducing the number of anti-ballistic missile systems would mean less pressure on the two sides to build more offensive missiles. That is why they were also able to agree to limit those numbers.
- Even so both sides retained the capacity to destroy the other with nuclear weapons.
- The Helsinki Agreement of 1975 emerged from the European Security Conference which met between 1973 and 1975. Canada, the USA, the USSR and 32 European countries met and agreed:
  1 to recognise the frontiers of Eastern Europe and Soviet influence over it
  2 that West Germany recognised East Germany
  3 to the exchange of cultural and trade links and technological information
  4 to respect human rights and allow freedom of travel across Europe.
- However, the USSR made little effort to improve its human rights record.

Marking

Basic description e.g. 'Both sides agreed to reduce missiles'. **[1–2]**
Either: Detail on just a few points
Or: A wide range of points without much explanation. **[3–4]**
Detailed description of several key points. **[5–6]**

(d) Key issue: Explanation of causation
- The Soviet invasion was a major reason for the breakdown of détente but was not the only reason.
- Détente was breaking down before the Soviet invasion of 1980 partly because of US suspicions over whether the USSR was keeping to the terms of SALT 1 and partly because of Western frustration over the Soviet Union's attitude to human rights.
- Tension was also increased because Brezhnev made it clear that the Cold War was not over. Certainly the USA and USSR maintained their rivalry in other parts of the world such as Angola and the Middle East.
- In the light of these tensions the invasion of

Afghanistan can be seen as a major additional cause for the ending of détente. Certainly its consequences seemed to re-start the Cold War in earnest.

- President Carter refused to agree to SALT II, boycotted the Moscow Olympics, started to rearm and banned US grain sales to the USSR.
- The election of President Reagan in the USA also destroyed détente. He viewed the Soviet Union as an 'evil empire' and accelerated US rearmament and the development of new weapons systems such as the neutron bomb, cruise missiles and the Strategic Defence Initiative.
- So the Soviet invasion of Afghanistan marked a key turning point in East–West relations and certainly after it détente seemed to be over. However, détente was already in decline before the invasion.

5 (a) **Key issue: Understanding of Source**
- Source I suggests there is now a new policy in Eastern Europe called the Sinatra Doctrine.
- From now on the countries of Eastern Europe will have the freedom to do things as they wish, without Soviet control. They will be able to do it 'their way' after the Sinatra song 'My Way'.

(b) **Key issue: Evaluation of reliability of a Source**
- Source I ought to be a reliable indicator of Soviet policy because the Source's author is a Soviet government spokesman in a good position, therefore, to comment on policy.
- He is also speaking in October 1989 at a time when the Soviet Union under Gorbachev was pursuing a policy of Glasnost or 'openness' which suggest this was more than just a propaganda statement.
- Gorbachev had made it clear that he would not use force against the countries of Eastern Europe and this had encouraged them to take a more independent line.
- Certainly this was happening in Hungary and Poland.
- However, the government spokesman calls this the Sinatra Doctrine, which may be just a joke playing on the American singer's famous song.
- Overall Source I gives a reliable indication of Soviet policy at this time even if the description is amusing.

(c) **Key issue: Understanding of an event**
- Glasnost means openness and refers to Gorbachev's attempt to restore faith in government by adopting a more open approach. This involved the ending of corruption and more freedom of speech. Dissidents would no longer be persecuted.
- Perestroika means restructuring and refers to Gorbachev's economic policies to improve the economy of the USSR. It involved allowing more capitalist enterprise and less state-control of the economy.

(d) **Key issue: Explanation of causation**
- Gorbachev's policies certainly did much to encourage change in Eastern Europe but these were not the only cause.
- Gorbachev's policies of perestroika and glasnost in the Soviet Union encouraged demands for similar policies in eastern European countries. Communist governments in Eastern Europe could also no longer rely on help from the Soviet Union in suppressing non-communist unrest because Gorbachev abandoned the Brezhnev Doctrine. Gorbachev's policies, especially perestroika, caused chaos in the Soviet Union and made it look weak.
- However, there was a range of other reasons for the growth of opposition in Eastern Europe which led to the collapse of communism:
- Many east European economies were inefficient and people wanted more freedom to run their own businesses and also wanted more consumer goods. Unemployment and economic difficulties had got worse in the 1980s which seemed to show communism wasn't working.
- People hated the censorship and propaganda in their countries and demanded freedom of speech and of the press. They also wanted freedom to practise religion.
- Finally there was a strong belief in nationalism in many East European countries and the people resented the control exerted by Moscow.
- Before Gorbachev had come to power, cracks had begun to appear in the Soviet system with the rise of Solidarity in Poland, but Gorbachev's policies were to encourage people in many East European states to protest their grievances, a situation which snowballed in 1989 and led to the collapse of

communist control. Gorbachev was very important then as the catalyst that opened the gates to revolution.

Marking

6 (a) **Key issue: Understanding of Source**
  • The photograph shows us that women were involved in the coal industry during the war.
  • The photograph shows us that women were able to take over many of the jobs that men would normally do – even heavy labour like shifting coal.
  • Women doing these jobs released male workers for the armed services.

Marking

 (b) **Key issue: Evaluation of the utility of a Source**
  • Source B is typical of the type of recruitment posters that were used to encourage men to volunteer for the war effort.
  • This poster plays on the idea that men would be doing what their wives and mothers would want them to do by volunteering. It is therefore a kind of emotional appeal to men's better nature.
  • Other posters played on other emotions such as nationalism and patriotism, or on the fear of being labelled a coward, or of duty.
  • Such posters are useful in illustrating the ways in which the Government attempted to recruit soldiers for the army, but do not necessarily tell us why they did volunteer. Often this was for reasons concerned with escape from the drudgery of factory life or peer pressure.

Marking

 (c) **Key issue: Use of Source and own knowledge to explain a development**
  • Source C indicates a major reason why the Government wanted to control the flow of information about the war. Lloyd George expresses the view that if people knew the truth about what life was really like on the Western Front people would not support the war effort.
  • However, this was not the only reason. Governments were concerned not just about issues of morale, but also had to have an eye to national security. They needed to control the flow of information in order to minimise the chances of the enemy getting hold of sensitive information about, for example, troop movements and locations, plans and proposed attacks. That is why soldiers' letters home had to be checked by their officers, for example.

Marking

 (d) **Key issue: Use of Source and own knowledge to assess an interpretation**
  • Source D supports the view that there was a problem of food supply during the First World War because it tells us about measures taken to increase food production. However, it does not tell us why these measures were taken.
  • Source D also says nothing about the introduction of rationing towards the end of the war which might indicate that Britain was near starvation.
  • Britain was dependent on imports of food from abroad and these were threatened by the U-boat campaigns waged from the start of the war. When the Germans declared unrestricted U-boat warfare in 1917 food supplies were threatened. In April 1917, for example, Britain had only about 6 weeks' supply of food left.
  • Thereafter things improved partly because of improved domestic production but mainly because the U-boat threat was increasingly well handled.
  • So the interpretation given could only be said to be true of April 1917. Before this date and after it, although there was some hardship and a lack of certain foodstuffs, Britain was not close to starvation.

Marking

7 (a) Key issue: Understanding of Source
- This source indicates that, contrary to popular beliefs about the 'Blitz spirit', it would seem that many people in the East End were bitter about the effects of bombing and that they would even take this out on members of the royal family.

(b) Key issue: Evaluation of the utility of a Source
- This source is quite useful as an indication of the measures taken by the Government to recruit women into the workforce and so release men for the armed services. Here the idea is that they can 'do their bit' by working in the arms factories to keep the soldiers and airmen supplied.
- This poster is typical of the posters which encouraged women to work on farms or help with transport, playing on a sense of patriotism and support for the armed services.
- However, the Source does not tell you how successful such recruitment campaigns were or whether women were able to replace men successfully. In fact thousands of women did volunteer for war work (Source C, for example indicates that 40 000 women volunteered for the Women's Land Army) and enabled Britain to fight the kind of total war which gave us the best chance of victory.

(c) Key issue: Use of Source and own knowledge to explain a key issue
- Source C tells us it was difficult to import food. This was because of the Battle of the Atlantic where German U-boats preyed on the merchant shipping bringing much needed food and other supplies to Britain. Britain could not feed herself and relied on imports getting through. By 1943 U-boats were sinking hundred of ships each year.
- Source C indicates some of the measures taken to help cope with this crisis – it tells us of the efforts made to use every available space to grow food and also the propaganda efforts made to encourage people to grow as much food as possible.

- This Source also indicates that the efforts were successful in increasing food production – suggesting food supply had doubled by 1944.
- This was crucial as Britain was not self-sufficient in food and needed to import. However, the Source does not tell the whole story. It does not mention rationing, for example.
- Unlike the First World War, in the Second World War rationing was introduced very early (1939) on a wide range of products. Rationing coupled with the measures indicated in the Source and victory in the Battle of the Atlantic meant that Britain coped well with the problems in food supply.
- Ironically the impact of rationing was to give many people a healthier and more balanced diet than they had enjoyed before the war.

(d) Key issue: Evaluation of an interpretation
- Winston Churchill was Prime Minister from 1940 until 1945 and his leadership was clearly very important in sustaining the British war effort.
- Source D is an extract from one of the many stirring and inspiring speeches made by Churchill during the war. His radio broadcasts had a major impact on stiffening British morale and deepening the resolve of British people to fight on. He seemed to epitomise the British bulldog spirit as the words of this speech indicate.
- However, Churchill was not just an inspiring speaker. He was an able politician and leader. He managed to keep a Cabinet made up from all the main political parties working together in support of the war effort.
- As important was the relationship he developed with the American president Roosevelt during the war. He persuaded him, for example, to keep Britain supplied before America joined the war. This was achieved, for example, through the Lease-Lend Act.
- Given Churchill's contribution it is difficult to see it as anything but vital, especially in the months when Britain was standing alone against Hitler from June 1940. Source D, of course, dates from this time, when Britain appeared on the verge of being invaded.

Answer to mock examination Paper 2

1 (a) **Key issue: Understanding of Source**
- Source A shows us that the Nazi Party gained increasing numbers of seats in the Reichstag after 1928 until July 1932, but then support dipped in November 1932 only to rise to its highest point in the election of March 1933.
- Source A also shows us that in September 1930 the Nazi party became the second largest party after the Social Democrats and that in July 1932 it became the largest party in the Reichstag.
- Despite these impressive election results, however, even in March 1933 the Nazi Party did not have an overall majority. Only if the Nationalists voted with it would it command a majority.

Marking

(b) **Key issue: Comparison of Sources**
- Sources B and C agree to some extent about why people might support the Nazi Party.
- Source C is a piece a Nazi election propaganda that suggests the German people, suffering from the effects of the Depression and, by implication, faced with the inability of the Weimar government to provide a solution to Germany's problems, should flock to Hitler as the only and the last hope of a better future.
- This is supported by Source B, where the headmistress gives her personal reasons for supporting the Nazis – she also views Hitler as the only hope for Germany. She says that only 'National Socialism offered any hope'.
- However, Source B provides an explanation of why she viewed the Nazis as the only hope for Germany. They were the only party actively combating the communists, whilst the 'middle class parties' were 'helpless' and could not cope with the economic crisis.
- What is implied by Source C, therefore, is said explicitly in Source B in relation to the economic problems facing Germany.

Marking

(c) **Key issue: Evaluating utility of a Source in context**
- Source B is useful in so far as it gives a number of reasons for supporting the Nazis at this time. Firstly people who were scared of a communist revolution might vote Nazi because they were the only party actively doing anything about the communist threat. Secondly, the middle-class parties like the Centre Party and the Social Democrats were useless and incapable of dealing with the problems caused by the depression. Thirdly the Nazi Party offered hope of a better future.
- However, this Source only tells us why this headmistress supported the Nazis. It does not tell us why others did.
- Clearly many people, especially from the middle classes, were afraid of the rise of the communist party (its proportion of the vote consistently rose between 1928 and 1932), and like the headmistress, many may have been attracted to the direct action taken by the Nazi Party.
- Clearly, also, with the inability of the Weimar government to stop the increase in unemployment, many were attracted to a party that seemed to promise a new way forward.
- However, this Source does not give a complete picture of why Hitler had so much success between 1928 and 1933. There were other reasons why the Nazis attracted support, such as their hatred for the Treaty of Versailles, his charismatic personality and the electrifying effect of his speeches, the carefully targeted propaganda of Goebbels and so on.

Marking

(d) **Key issue: Assessment of an interpretation**
- This cartoon indicates that Germans voted Nazi on 5 March 1933 because they were forced to or feared for their lives if they didn't.
- There is some evidence to support this interpretation. For example, after the Reichstag Fire,

Hitler declared an emergency and used the fire as an excuse to arrest communists. Members of the SA policed the polling stations and intimidated voters as they came to vote. Such intimidation may help to explain why so many voted Nazi on 5 March 1933. Hitler was also in a powerful position, having been made Chancellor in January 1933. As such he had control of the police which could also be used to intimidate other parties and voters.

- However, this Source does not provide a complete explanation of why people voted for the Nazis. After all, the Nazis were the largest party in the Reichstag already and so had already won considerable support from the German people.
- The Source is also a British interpretation of the election and is clearly biased against Hitler, portraying him as little more than a gangster. This makes this hard to believe as a full interpretation.

(e) Key issue: Explanation of an event

- Hitler was made Chancellor in January 1933 and by August 1934 he had made himself dictator (Fuhrer) of Germany. They were a number of key stages by which Hitler consolidated his power over Germany.
- The first was the Reichstag Fire which enabled Hitler to declare an emergency and rule by decree in the run up to the 5 March election.
- The result of that election was crucial. It meant that with the support of the Nationalists and with the exclusion of the Communists he could pass legislation which would give him dictatorial powers. This was achieved when the Reichstag passed the Enabling Law, which gave Hitler the power to rule by decree for four years.
- Hitler quickly set about using these powers to eliminate possible sources of opposition. Trade unions were banned and other political parties were prohibited. The media was controlled by Goebbels as Minister for Enlightenment and Propaganda. In these ways freedom of speech was curtailed and opposition was starved of the oxygen of publicity.
- In 1934 he turned on potential opposition from within the Nazi movement, especially that surrounding the leader of the SA Ernst Röhm. He and a range of other critics and opponents were disposed of in the Night of the Long Knives in June 1934.
- One reason he had turned on the SA was to win the support of the army. This was achieved and when the aged president Hindenburg finally died in August 1934 Hitler was not only able to declare himself Führer of Germany but also got the army to take a personal oath of loyalty to him.

2 (a) Key issue: Understanding of a Source

- This source shows the initiation ceremony of a new member into the Ku Klux Klan. We can see in the photograph the distinctive outfits of the KKK, the white gowns and hoods. These were to ensure the anonymity of members and give the appearance of secrecy.
- The new member is kept blindfold until he has been initiated. The nature of the ceremony appears almost religious with the new member being asked to swear an oath of loyalty.
- We can also see the American flag, evidence of the KKK view that they represented 'true Americans'.

(b) Key issue: Comparison of Sources

- Source C indicates forcefully that the KKK viewed blacks as a threat to the 'white supremacy' referred to in Source B. We are told that the Negro was accused of killing a white woman and the punishment meted out to the black is brutal.
- Source B can be used to corroborate the hatred of blacks because of the question asked of new members about striving for white supremacy. However, Source B gives an indication that the concerns of the KKK went well beyond hatred of blacks and included Jews and other non-Christians. It also included all immigrants as indicated by the phrase 'native-born'.

(c) Key issue: Evaluation of the utility of a Source in context

- Source C indicates that racism was not just confined to the southern states and rural areas where the KKK was strongest, but that it was also present in northern cities like Chicago.
- The extract represents the views of the journalist and is clearly heavily prejudiced against blacks. The

Source uses a range of abusive terms to describe blacks – 'unsanitary', 'irresponsible', 'vicious'. However, the fact that this was an article in *The Chicago Property Owners Journal* indicates that the views expressed were likely to be those of the wealthier white propertied classes in Chicago, presumably the intended audience.

- However, it would be dangerous to draw definite conclusions from this one Source, although it does fit in with what is known about Chicago after the First World War. The city experienced a number of race riots and racial tensions were very high.

Marking

(d) Key issue: Evaluation of an interpretation

- The view expressed in this Source commands respect because it is from an historian who has studied the Ku Klux Klan in detail and written a history of the movement.
- He suggests that the Klan appealed directly to white-native, anglo-saxon protestants (WASPs) in the USA who felt threatened by the changing times and the flood of non-'WASP' immigration which seemed to threaten traditional ways of life.
- Certainly the KKK was strongest in the rural areas away from the 'corruption and vice' of the big cities. The KKK also stood for the defence of what it called 'true Americanism' which was threatened by Catholics, anarchists and communist ideas.
- But the Klan was also strongest in the southern states well away from the northern cities. The main target of the KKK appeared to be blacks as indicated by Source C.
- What the Source does not indicate is that many of the 4 million or so who joined the Klan in the 1920s did so because it appeared to bring a kind of purpose and a sense of excitement into their lives.
- On balance, however, this Source is an accurate reflection of why many Americans joined the Klan.

Marking

(e) Key issue: Understanding of a historical period

- The USA experienced an economic boom in the 1920s in a whole range of areas. These included motor cars, buildings and roads, as well as consumer goods such as telephones, typewriters, radios, fridges and vacuum cleaners.
- The boom in the car industry was particularly strong and the number of cars on the road trebled during the 1920s, the most common being the Model T Ford.
- The boom in the motor industry stimulated other industries like glass, steel, rubber and oil.
- There was also a boom in the electricity industry as its use spread across the USA in industry and homes.
- In economic terms, therefore, there is strong evidence of a boom.
- The economic boom also led to a boom in other areas of life. For example, the 1920s saw the film industry take off as millions of Americans went to the cinema every week. The sale of radios meant that the number of radio stations increased and sport became more important as all could now listen to the commentaries on games.
- However, not all areas of the economy nor society experienced the boom. Two groups in particular were left out – farmers and the blacks.
- Agricultural production had boomed in the war years, but in the 1920s American agriculture was suffering from over-production resulting in low or non-existent profit margins. This lack of profitability hit the small farmer and sharecropper hardest and many barely scraped a living from the land.
- Many sharecroppers were also black. Blacks had always been at the bottom of the social and economic pile and the 1920s were no exception. Some sought to escape the poverty of their existence on the cotton and tobacco plantations of the south by moving to the northern cities but often life was not much better there.
- A survey in 1929 found that over 18 million Americans lived in real poverty and that the benefits of the boom were enjoyed mainly by the already rich. In 1929 the richest 5% of the population enjoyed over a third of the nation's wealth.
- So overall, although the USA produced more than it had ever done in the 1920s, the boom was not enjoyed by all sectors of the economy or society.

Marking

3 (a) Key issue: Understanding of Source

- Source A tells us that girls' education involved a long school day (8 am to 6 pm) and that there were sometimes evening sessions.
- Sport played a large role in the school day with at least 4 hours per day.
- Apart from subjects you would expect (German, history, geography) there were subjects like race studies, ideology and eugenics – reflecting Hitler's aims for indoctrinating the youth of Germany.
- Girls also studied domestic science and health biology perhaps to prepare them for their role as wives and mothers.

(b) Key issue: Use of Source and own knowledge to explain a development

- In Source B Hitler makes clear that he wants boys (he appears to be talking about boys, given the final sentence) to be the instruments for making his 'new world'. Education must therefore eliminate weakness and make them into fearless, active and brutal young men, indifferent to pain and incapable of independent thought.
- This view reflects the approach adopted towards boys' education and the hard experience of the Order Castles and Adolf Hitler schools designed for the future elite. These young men were to be the fathers of the master race, the foundation of a 1000 year Reich, indoctrinated with the ideas of racial purity and superiority and obedience to the Fuhrer. They would need to be the warriors for the future wars.

(c) Key issue: Understanding of a key issue

- Hitler believed woman's role was that of wife and mother, rather than that of independent career women equal to men. His policies reflected these views.
- Girls were to be brought up to accept their role in life – to be fit wives and mothers of the Aryan master race. Education placed great emphasis on these areas.
- Women were discouraged from working and from wearing make-up. The ideal was a plain blond country girl.
- Women were encouraged to get married and bear as many children as possible. Incentives were provided for this, such as marriage loans (which didn't have to be repaid as long as the couple had four or more children), medals for prolific mothers and other honours.
- Single women could also enrol in special SS brothels to mate with Aryan men.

(d) Key issue: Evaluation of success

- Economic policy between 1933 and 1939 was dominated by two plans – the 'New Plan' devised and administered by Dr Schacht up to 1937, and the Four Year Plan drawn up in 1936 and run by Hermann Goering.
- The main aims of the New Plan were to reduce unemployment, to build up armaments and to make Germany self-sufficient (autarky). These priorities had to be balanced against the demand for consumer goods to keep people happy.
- Unemployment was brought down in two main ways, by public works such as the building of the German motorway system (*Autobahnen*), hospitals and schools, and by rearmament. The latter had the greater impact. In 1935 Hitler reintroduced conscription to produce an army of over 1 million by 1938. In numerical terms the attack on unemployment seems to have been successful, the figures had fallen from 5 million in 1933 to practically zero in 1939. However, the latter figures did not include women or Jews.
- Self-sufficiency (autarky) in raw materials was a main aim of Hitler's Four Year Plan. More raw materials were produced (coal, iron, steel) and where Germany did not possess resources, synthetic or ersatz products were produced (such as ersatz rubber, textiles and fuel). New factories were built, like the Hermann Goering works.
- Although production increased, however, the Plan was very expensive, requiring massive state investment and did not fulfil all its aims. Germany was still importing one third of its raw materials in 1939.
- The Four Year Plan also put great emphasis on rearmament and again there were some impressive jumps in production. By 1939 Germany was spending nearly 40% of its national wealth on rearmament and between 1936 and 1938 production of explosives more than doubled.
- Overall it seems that Hitler's economic policies, whilst falling short of hopes and targets, did have considerable success in some areas – as in reducing unemployment.

(e) Key issue: Evaluation of success

- The Nazis had a good deal of success in eliminating opposition but did not completely succeed.
- The Enabling Law of 1933 gave Hitler the power he needed to get rid of possible opposition. He used the powers the law gave him to abolish the trade unions and other political parties.
- In the Night of the Long Knives, in June 1934, Hitler dealt with possible opposition from within the Nazi party when Ernst Röhm and others were killed.
- The Nazis also stifled potential opposition by imposing strict censorship of all media, from sculpture to newspapers.
- The SS and Gestapo were used to create an atmosphere of fear which prevented many from expressing opposition. Fear of the early morning raid, of spies and informers and of the concentration camp kept the people under control.
- However, despite all these measures there was some opposition. Some Germans expressed opposition in small ways, by 'forgetting' to do the German salute, for example. One common form of opposition was the telling of anti-Nazi jokes.
- Others in the Churches, for example, were more open in their opposition. For example, Pastor Grüeber protected Jews; Cardinal Galen criticised Nazi policies, and Pastor Neimöller criticised Hitler's 'German Christians'.
- Young people expressed opposition in the 'Swing' movement by listening to banned music and flouting Nazi 'rules' of social behaviour.
- Some students expressed more direct opposition by issuing anti-Nazi pamphlets. One such movement was the White Rose movement.
- There were also plots against Hitler, the most famous of which resulted in the failed attempt to blow Hitler up in July 1944.
- This plot also showed how opposition grew during the war, especially after the tide turned against the Germans in 1943. One example of such opposition was the activity of the Edelweiss Pirates, some of whom were executed for killing the head of the Cologne Gestapo.
- Overall, whilst the Nazis were able to contain and eliminate much opposition they were unable to crush it all.

Marking

Either: Simple descriptive, narrative coverage
Or: Simple narrative implying reasons for success. **[1–3]**
Either: One relevant point made in detail
Or: Narrative implying analysis of success
Or: Several points made analysing success, but without detail. **[4–8]**
Either: Several points made with detail analysing success
Or: A selective and organised account emphasising some arguments both ways. **[9–12]**
Well-argued, sustained argument making several points and analysing success, arriving at a reasoned balanced judgement. **[13–15]**

4 (a) Key issue: Understanding of Source

- This Source illustrates the type of extremes and desperation many Americans were forced to during the Depression.
- Unemployed and often homeless, men were forced to find food where they could, in this case by raiding the dustbins of restaurants.

Marking

Just repeats information from the Source. **[1]**
An inference from the results, used to explain the purpose of the education. **[2–3]**

(b) Key issue: Use of Source and own knowledge to explain an issue

- This cartoon is criticising the New Deal by suggesting it was a waste of billions of dollars of taxpayers' money. The 'New Deal' pump was so badly designed and full of holes that most of the money was wasted before it got to where it was intended to go.
- This was one of the criticisms made by Republican opponents. They also criticised the New Deal because of the degree of state intervention in the economy and because it made Americans dependent on the Government for hand-outs.
- Businessmen objected to the support given to trade unions by the New Deal and others believed the Federal government was interfering in areas over which State governments should have control. Conservatives believed the New Deal was leading America along the road to socialism.
- At the other end of the political spectrum, the New Deal was also criticised for not doing enough. Father Coughlin set up the National Union for Social Justice which demanded more help for those affected by the Depression and Governor Huey Long campaigned for more extreme reforms.

Marking

Simple description of criticisms, with general coverage. **[1–2]**
Either: One fact developed in detail
Or: Several facts not explained in detail. **[3–5]**
Several facts, explained in detail. **[6–7]**

(c) Key issue: Understanding of an event

- The Hundred Days refers to the first hundred days when Roosevelt was in office. During this time he took a large number of measures to combat the effects of the Depression.
- Measures included the cutting of government spending on wages for government employees, the ending of prohibition and the setting up of a number of 'alphabet agencies'.
- These included the AAA (Agricultural Adjustment Act) which controlled agricultural production, the CCC (Civilian Conservation Corps) which provide work for young men, the CWA (Civil Works Administration) which provided jobs on public projects such as building schools and roads, the FERA (Federal Emergency Relief Administration) which provided cash for poor relief and the NIRA (National Industrial Recovery Act) which was to provide jobs and stimulate the economy.

(d) Key issue: Evaluation of success

- Many people did benefit from the New Deal.
- The New Deal, for example, through agencies like the CCC and the PWA, helped reduce unemployment from nearly 13 million in 1933 to under 8 million by 1937.
- Millions received poor relief from New Deal agencies, including food, shelter and clothing. Social security schemes helped people throughout this period.
- Construction work on roads and dams (such as the Tennesee Valley scheme) stimulated industry.
- Workers benefited from the improvement in their rights and working conditions under the NRA codes and the Wagner Act.
- Farmers benefited from the working of the AAA. Farm incomes rose during the 1930s.
- More generally, the New Deal restored morale in America and gave Americans hope after the dark days of the Depression.
- However, not everyone benefited from the New Deal.
- Unemployment remained a problem throughout the 1930s despite the New Deal. In 1938 figures rose again. This problem was only ended with the coming of war in 1941.
- Employers resented the restrictions placed on them by the NRA and the Wagner Act. There were violent strikes and clashes in the later 1930s.
- Small farmers and sharecroppers got little benefit from the AAA and they were hit hard by the drought of 1934–35 which created the dustbowls in some states like Kansas.
- Not all the poor benefited. For example, the Social Security Act did not apply to domestic servants and farmworkers.
- Black Americans also failed to benefit. No New Deal laws sought to help blacks or improve their civil rights.
- Overall, the benefits outweigh the disadvantages, however, and the New Deal must be judged at least a partial success.

(e) Key issue: Explanation of consequences

- The Wall Street Crash had a devastating effect on the US economy.
- Clearly the Crash had severe effects on many Americans because they lost fortunes they had invested on the Stock Market. The losses for the three weeks from 23 October 1929 are estimated at between 30 and 40 billion dollars. Investors were forced to sell their property and homes and some resorted to suicide. However, less than 1% of the population owned shares and were directly affected in this way.
- The collapse in share prices also had a devastating effect on industry. Businesses found that their paper value collapsed which meant they could no longer raise the money to invest in new machinery or finance loans. For example, the value of General Motors in mid-November 1929 was less than a quarter of its value in September.
- The Crash affected the vast majority of Americans because the collapse of the Stock Market brought much more deep-rooted problems in the economy to the fore. The economy was already slowing down before the Crash. The effect of the Crash was to turn a slow-down into a collapse.
- Money for investment dried up. Production was cut and workers were laid off. In this way an economic downward spiral was begun. As workers were laid off they could no longer afford to buy the products industry made. This meant industry cut production and more workers were laid off and so the spiral continued. Well over 100 000 businesses a year went bust during the Depression and the number of unemployed escalated to nearly 13 millions.
- As the effects of the Crash developed, people who had money in savings withdrew them and banks called in loans. Because many businesses could not afford to pay back loans, many banks failed – over 2000 in 1931.
- For these reasons then, the effects of the Wall Street Crash were devastating.

Index